Twelve Days

Vita is not a born adventurer: 'I hate mountains' and 'I hate tents', she exclaims, while Harold, 'characteristically' forgetting his jacket and instead wearing the local Bakhtiari cape, manages to look no more romantic than a penguin.

But they are, after all, following the route Alexander is thought to have taken to India, and there are rare iris and tulip bulbs to be searched for.

Amidst the inconvenience of the journey, Vita reflects on the lives of the nomads who must wearily cross these mountains year after year. She would prefer to be a solitary, to stay put in this isolated part of the world—and this leads her to some interesting comparisons between the East and the West.

She considers how Persia (modern Iran) is on the verge of developing in a Western fashion. Oil has just been discovered, the first roads are being built. There is still the chance, she dreams, of establishing an ideal and enlightened state. And with prescience she warns of the calamity that would overtake the country if the mullahs ever achieved power.

John Julius Norwich has drawn on *Twelve Days* in *A Taste for Travel*, his anthology of 'the most fascinating, moving, amusing, extraordinary and awe-inspiring pieces of travel writing down the ages'.

D1253798

SOME OTHER BOOKS PUBLISHED BY MICHAEL HAAG

The Traveller's Journey is Done, *by Dilys Powell*
Alexandria: A History and a Guide, *by E M Forster, with an
introduction by Lawrence Durrell*
Libyan Sands: Travel in a Dead World, *by R A Bagnold*
Crusader Castles of the Levant, *by Robin Fedden and
John Thomson*
Journey to the Orient, *by Gérard de Nerval*

Please send for our complete list:
*Michael Haag Limited
PO Box 369
London NW3 4ER
England*

Twelve Days
An Account of a Journey Across the Bakhtiari Mountains of South-western Persia

Vita Sackville-West

MICHAEL HAAG

Copyright © 1928 by Vita Sackville-West

Cover design by Colin Elgie

Printed in Great Britain by litho at
The Bath Press, Lower Bristol Road, Bath BA2 3BL

Published 1987 by Michael Haag Limited, PO Box 369,
London NW3 4ER, England

ISBN 0 902743 43 0

TO

HAROLD NICOLSON

" Grant me however this one favour: permit me to take a holiday, like one of these men of indolent minds, who are wont to feast themselves on their own thoughts whenever they travel alone. Such persons, you know, before they have found out any means of effecting their wishes, pass that by, to avoid the fatigue of thinking whether such wishes are practicable or not, and assume that what they desire is already theirs."   PLATO's *Republic*.

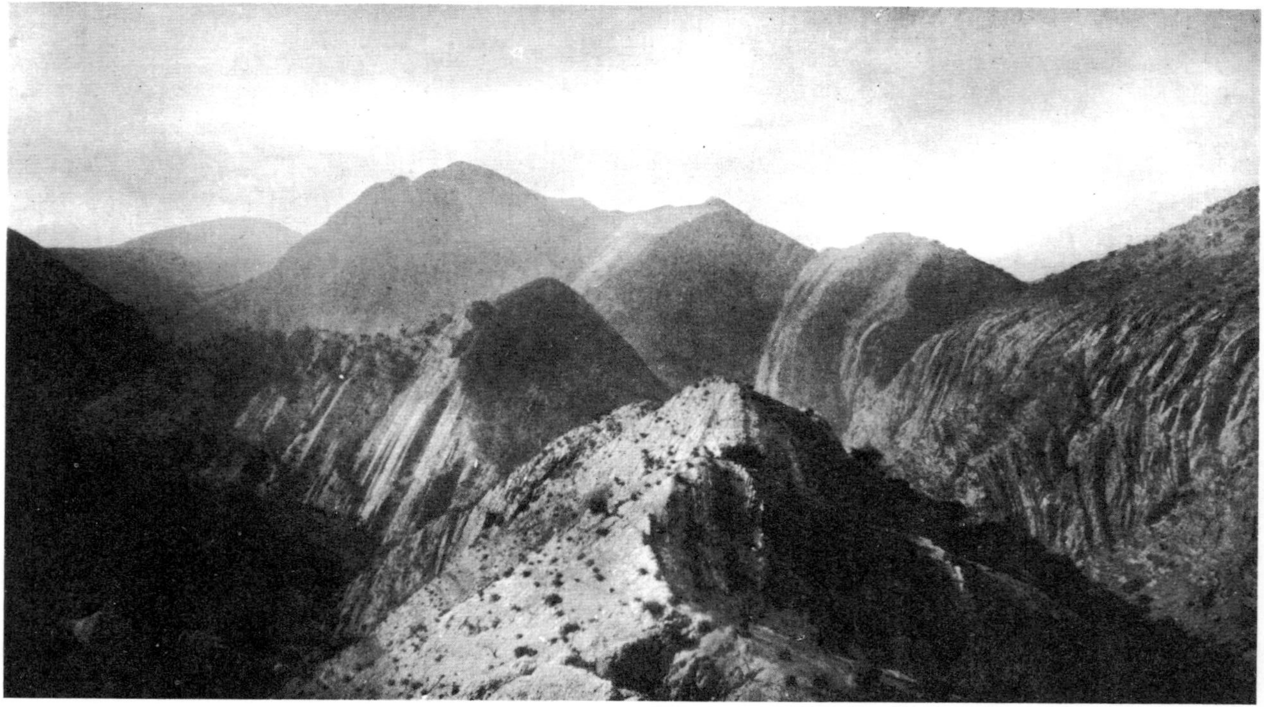

BAKHTIARI COUNTRY

RUINED CARAVANSERAI AT SHALIL

A WANDERING DERVISH, DEH DIZ

I

For a long time I believed that it would be impossible to make a book out of these experiences; I could see no shape in them, no pleasing curve; nothing but a series of anti-climaxes, and too much repetition of what I had done, and written down, before. Yet I was loath to let the whole thing go unrecorded. Was it for this that I had gone footsore, cold, hot, wet, hungry? climbed up, and scrambled down? covered all those miles? looked at all those goats? Surely not. There must be a possible book in it somewhere. The book was always in my mind, teasing at me, and little by little, as time receded, it began to take shape, a meaning began to rise up out of the welter, a few definite conclusions which really had some bearing on half-formulated ideas; besides, the fingers which have once grown accustomed to a pen soon itch to hold one again: it is necessary to write, if the days are not to slip emptily by. How else, indeed, to clap the net over the butterfly of the moment? for the moment passes, it is forgotten; the mood is gone; life itself is gone. That is where the writer scores over his fellows: he catches the changes of his mind on the hop. Growth is exciting; growth is dynamic and alarming.

Growth of the soul, growth of the mind; how the observation of last year seems childish, superficial; how this year,—even this week,—even with this new phrase,—it seems to us that we have grown to a new maturity.   It may be a fallacious persuasion, but at least it is stimulating, and so long as it persists, one does not stagnate.

I look back as through a telescope, and see, in the little bright circle of the glass, moving flocks and ruined cities.

II

THERE they are, a long way off, and looking at the map of Asia, a kind of awe comes over me that I should be able to visualise the place represented by a name in cold black print. I know how vast are the spaces which on the map cover one inch. I know how high and arduous are the mountains which on the map deepen only into a stronger shade of brown. I think of life going on there, the same to-day as when I, so briefly, brushed past it. The nomads are on the move; their black tents dot the plain; the fierce dogs rush out barking, as a wild figure on horseback gallops up and flings himself from the saddle. At night the black tents cower between red fires. It is exactly the same for them this year as last, and the days which stand out so vividly for me were for them merely the uncalendared days of ordinary existence. Malamir to-day scorches in the sun. Do-Pulan sleeps in the shadow of the hill by the banks of the Karoun. In the dripping gorge below Gandom Kar the Crown Imperials rear their brilliant orange among the rocks.

The Bakhtiari country. "Bakhtiari", says the *Encyclopædia Britannica*, "one of the great nomad tribes of Persia." It goes on to mention the Haft-lang and the Chahar-lang as the two main divisions of the tribe; it records a stormy and blood-stained history. "Here," says Lord Curzon, "in a *mise en scène* which unites all the elements of natural grandeur,—snowy crags, rugged hills, mountain ravines,—are the *yelaks* or summer quarters of the tribes." Alas, how bleak and brief is the written word.

One of the great nomad tribes of Persia, the Bakhtiari are Lurs, but who the Lurs are and whence they came, as Lord Curzon says, is one of the unsolved riddles of history. "A people without a history, a literature, or even a tradition," he says, "presents a phenomenon in face of which science stands abashed. Are they Turks? Are they Persians? Are they Semites? All three hypotheses have been urged. They appear to belong to the same ethnical group as the Kurds, their neighbours on the north; nor does their language, which is a dialect of Persian, differ materially from the Kurdish tongue. On the other hand, they consider it an insult to be confounded with the Kurds, whom they call Leks; and the majority of writers have agreed in regarding them as the veritable relics of the old Aryan or Iranian stock, who preceded Arabs, Turks, and Tartars in the land. Whilst, however, we may accept this as the most probable hypothesis, and may even be led thereby to regard with heightened interest these last survivals of an illustrious stock, we are not compelled to endorse the conjectural connection of Bakhtiari with Bactria, which has been propounded by some writers, or to localise their ancestral home. (Some have gone so far as to base on this resemblance the assertion that the Bakhtiari are the relics of one of the Greek colonies left by Alexander in Asia, an hypothesis for which the further support is claimed of a similarity in the Greek and Bakhtiari national dances.) It is sufficient to believe that they are Aryans by descent, and to know that they have lived for centuries in their present mountains." Rawlinson, who travelled among the Bakhtiari, characterised them as " the most wild and barbarous of all the inhabitants of Persia "; but we, making plans for our expedition, were less interested in the history and nature of the tribe than in the road which we should have to travel.

We had spent many an evening in Teheran, poring over maps and discussing our journey across the Bakhtiari country. It had not been easy to get information; the maps were most inadequate; there seemed to be no books in Teheran available on the subject of more recent date than Sir Henry Layard's, which related an expedition undertaken in 1840, nor were there any Europeans in Teheran who had travelled over the Bakhtiari Road. We had to rely on a few letters, none of which were very reassuring. A young officer in the Indian Army wrote that he had never been so exhausted in his life, and other accounts spoke of precipices and crazy bridges, and swirling rivers to ford,—all of which, save for the wail about exhaustion, proved to be completely misleading. Travellers like to exaggerate the perils they have run; so, not to fall into the common error, I say at the outset that never at any moment were our brittle limbs in the slightest danger. The Bakhtiari Road, certainly, is not for those who like a country stroll; but it may be undertaken by the most cowardly if they are but sufficiently active. Indeed, the only intrepidity which we displayed was our determination to go despite the romantic discouragement which we received.

The Bakhtiari Khans living in Teheran gave a different account of their own country. Either they were loath to acknowledge that their famous Road was not made of asphalt, or else in the amiable mendacious way of the East they wished to flatter our ears with pleasant hearing; I remember that on asking one of them if it was possible to ride over the Road, or if one must go on foot, I obtained the startling reply, " Ride? but you can go in a motor! " Now this was not true. It was indeed magnificently untrue: it was a lie on the grand scale. By courtesy it is known as the Bakhtiari Road, but actually it is a trail, a track, which leads, now up, now down, over wild and mountainous country; and as for wheeled traffic, no one could push even a wheelbarrow over it. My neighbour at dinner must have known how soon and how thoroughly his words would be disproved; but after the manner of his race he no doubt thought it more agreeable to produce a comfortable impression at the moment, leaving the future to take care of itself. Familiar with the Persian habit, I forbore from argument. Sitting there at dinner in the sumptuous house of the rich Khans, the Road seemed remote enough; a large façade of civilisation seemed to have been erected, a façade built up out of the French language, poker and poker chips, and the innovation by which the Persians

laid aside their *kolahs* after dinner; but behind it rose
the mountains which turned all this sophistication to
a sham. The Salon pictures of 1880, the candelabra,
the ormolu, even the acetylene lamps on the table—
giving a glaring white light and known frequently
to explode—could not wholly eliminate the sense of a
certain primitive, feudal organisation in the background,
—the source of wealth, the domain and territory where
our suave hosts abandoned their pretences, and went
back to the brutalities they had known as little boys.
Those carpets hanging on the walls, those amorini,
that representation of Omar accepting a draught of
wine from the cup-bearer—those had been woven by
women of the tribes, rocking a cradle with one hand
while with the other they threaded the swift shuttle.
Soft and polite, our hosts had, elsewhere, a complete,
separate existence. They had no intention of talking
about it. Of course not. The Road? The Bakhtiari Road? Why, you can go by motor. Who
among us betrays his family secrets to a stranger?
All is for the best; and we talk least about what we
know most intimately. In fact, the more glibly a
man talks, the more you may mistrust his knowledge.
Complete, detailed intimacy begets reticence. The
mountains rise in the background, willy-nilly; but they
are blocked out by the poker-chips; it is the façade
which we all put up.

Little by little, our expedition began to take shape.
The dates were settled and a letter despatched to
Isfahan ordering tents and mules. Our Bakhtiari
friends in Teheran promised us an escort. (An

escort? Here was a hint, surely, that the Road was not quite the Route Nationale they would have us believe?) We dragged out our camp equipment, and sorted it on the landing at the top of the stairs: two beds, two sleeping-bags, a Rawkee chair, a folding table, a green canvas bucket, two felt-covered water-bottles, a blue tin basin. My camera. My films, in tin cylinders. An amphora full of apricot jam. So much, and no more, would Harold Nicolson and I provide. Our dogs nosed round uneasily, scenting departure. Meanwhile, the caravan increased: to Harold Nicolson, Gladwyn Jebb, and myself, the original three, were added Copley Amory from the American Legation in Teheran, and Lionel Smith, who by letter announced his intention of coming up from Baghdad to join us; so that altogether we were five Europeans setting out on the Bakhtiari Road.

III

THE new moon rose in a cloudless sky at Isfahan on the evening before we set out. We sat in the garden watching Venus and the slip of moon travel together between two tall poplars, in a silence broken only by the croaking of frogs and the distant cries coming from the town. Harold Nicolson and I had just returned from Shiraz, the others had come down from Teheran, bringing our fortnightly post with them. Harold Nicolson was in a dejected frame of mind, for in the post-bag he had received the proofs of *Some People*, and I was only just in time to stop him from sending Messrs. Constable a cable to cancel publication. "It's *too* feeble," he said, standing with the telegram ready written out in his hand, "I can't possibly let it appear." Very grudgingly he gave me the second set of proofs to read. "You take the responsibility then," he said when a few hours later I met him with expostulations; "I wash my hands of the thing." I said I would take the responsibility.

So we sat rather sulkily in the garden watching Venus and the new moon. The month was April, the evening air warm and milky. It had been raining;

the smell of the wet earth came up to us as it so often does in England, but so rarely in Persia. Little gold and purple irises grew all along the path, on the edges of the irrigation stream. The gardener had told me that the bulbs came from Gandom Kar, on the Bakhtiari Road, and I had made a resolution to find them there; but it was not of the Bakhtiari Road that I was now thinking. My thoughts were washing lazily round in a sea of impressions; coming up to the surface in a series of little pictures. Nearly a thousand miles of motoring had given me plenty of pretext for idle dreaming. We had passed through Isfahan only a short while ago, and now were returned there; but I for one did not feel myself to be quite the same person: I felt that something had been added to me—something which I could never quite communicate to anybody else; an enrichment. It was as though my eyes could see a new colour which nobody else could see. My companions, doubtless, saw a new colour too; but it could not be precisely the same colour as mine: *that* was a personal possession, incommunicable (alas and thank God) in words.

Those floating pictures. Would they fade with time?

An absurd picture started the series: ourselves in the market-place of a brown mud village, the ground strewn with our intimate possessions, hair-brushes, sponges, pyjamas, while two religious processions passed by, howling at the top of their voices, but neglected by the villagers, who preferred (small blame to them) to watch us. Our luggage car, a Ford, had broken down some fifteen miles back, and after pushing it for those fifteen miles with the nose of the other car, we had decided to abandon it in the village and pack the essentials of our luggage on to our beautiful brand-new Dodge. A ludicrous spectacle we must have presented, bending over our *disjecta membra* in the market-place at Kumisheh in Persia.

Then floated up into my mind a vision of brown villages, a whole string of villages, up a wide valley, perhaps a mile from the track over which we travelled; brown villages among poplars, with blue domes of little mosques, and round pigeon-towers, and blossom, blossom, blossom. Blossom frothing over the walls, pink blossom, white blossom, like gauze, like a light cloud tossed up into the air to remain caught among the poplars and the blue domes. The villages followed the course of a stream, a long belt of fruitfulness; alas that we had no time to strike across the valley and enter them. They remained nameless for me, nameless and seen only from afar, in their cloud of ethereal unreality.

Then we had come to Yezd-i-Khast, that fantastic grey eyrie overhanging a chasm. Pierre Loti compared it to the abode of sea birds; Gobineau, to a bee-hive. On one side it is flush with the plain, but on the other it rises sheer up from a dry river-bed, a skeleton-coloured cliff of a town, pierced with windows like the eye-sockets of a skull, and beetling with wooden balconies and platforms that threaten to fall at any moment into the canyon below. It is difficult to see where the natural rock ends and the houses

begin.   The whole structure seems to be hooked and
hitched together, in defiance, as Pierre Loti rightly
said, of all the laws of equilibrium and common sense;
rickety, ramshackle, crazy, yet of untraceable antiquity.   No architect hitched it there; it grew, as
though the rock had sprouted upward, as though the
original rock-dwellings had produced and transformed
themselves into the semblance of sun-baked hovels.
An air of uncompromising violence hangs about it.
Its inhabitants must surely differ from other men.   In
the heart of this strange structure lurks a mosque, split
from roof to floor by earthquake.   Why did the earthquake not precipitate the whole folly into the ravine?
Like an old ship, whose timbers creak and complain,
it probably enjoys unlimited flexibility.   But it was
not without misgiving that we ascended to one of those
upper rooms.

Few travellers spend the night at Yezd-i-Khast.
They usually push on to Abadeh, where there is a
telegraph-house, and the telegraph-clerk and his wife
to look after them.   We, however, delayed by the
misadventure with the Ford, came to Yezd-i-Khast at
sunset and preferred to share our bed with the chickens
than to cross the barren plains after nightfall in a
solitary motor.   If one is benighted in Persia one
makes the best of it; but no reasonable traveller ex-
poses himself and his belongings if he can help it.
He is not necessarily a coward, but he remembers that
story of the missionary on the Bushire road who was
left with nothing but a tail-coat—which he wore back
to front—in which to make his entry into Bushire.

We asked if we could have a room in Yezd-i-Khast. The whole population had of course gathered round us, gazing greedily, but they were kept in check by an authoritative person in a green robe, the colour of an unripe lemon, who appeared to be the headman of the village and, as such, entitled to whatever profit the foreigners were likely to bring. We could, most certainly we could, have a room. Stiff, cramped—for we were five, plus luggage, in the motor now that the overflow of the Ford had been squashed into and on to the Dodge,—we followed our host through the throng of villagers. I was, and I say it with apologetic shame, the least cramped of the five, for it was I who drove the motor, and so could neither be asked to prop my legs up on petrol tins, nor to balance a suitcase on my knees. On the other hand, I had to keep a sharp look-out for what the French so elegantly call *les inégalités du terrain*,—no light matter in Persia, where an apparently perfect stretch of desert track is apt to be broken by a ditch crossing the road, invisible until you are right on it, or where the going is so bad that for twenty miles at a stretch the speedometer twitches round the mark at five miles an hour. Nevertheless, I think I had the best of it. Stiff, cramped, therefore, we followed our host into the labyrinth of his house. Like all Persian houses, it was lavishly populated. Women, children, chickens, dogs, goats, donkeys, meandered at their ease through vague enclosures which might have been rooms or might have been stables, the floor made of earth, straw, and dung, the walls of the usual sun-dried mud. The women peeped and tittered as we passed; a very old woman tried to bribe us before she would unbar a door, but our host swept her aside in his lordly way. It was dark, and some crouching women were cooking over a red fire in a corner. We ascended by a flight of open steps to the roof level. Over the distant mountains the last bars of sunset slashed the sky with blood. The plain beneath was black as a dark sea. A faint music of camel bells rose up to us. This was our roof; our private belvedere in Yezd-i-Khast.

The room into which our host proudly showed us was tiny; a little mud cell; in actual measurements it could not have exceeded eight feet square. It had an opening looking towards the east, a casement without glass, but closed by a wooden shutter; and a door barred by a wooden bolt of such ingenuity that, having locked ourselves in for the night, it took all our wits to let ourselves out again in the morning. An arrangement of bolt, socket, and groove scooped in the clay wall; to this day I have no idea how it worked. There we were, in Yezd-i-Khast, dangled over a deep ravine, with a cut-throat villain for a host—for all we knew— and only just enough room to lay ourselves down for the night.

Down in the village street stood our motor, the ceiling light switched on, brilliantly illuminating the interior, and inside it, oblivious to the crowd that pressed against the windows, reclined our English mechanic (he who had driven the Ford until its collapse), reading Gibbon.

We were aroused in the morning by a knocking

on the door and the voice of our host: "The dawn has come," he said, "and the sun is rising." So noble and high-sounding a summons brought us to our feet. Scrambling out of our sleeping-bags, in the cramped disorder of the little room, we unbarred the wooden shutter and looked out towards the east. Below us the ravine lay, still in shadow, rising on the opposite side to the level of the plain. The plain stretched away, dark and wide, to a range of jagged hills across the horizon. The sun had not yet appeared, but the whole east was lambent with his near presence; the hills stood up, sombre shapes, against a saffron heaven bruised and streaked with narrow purple clouds, protean. The camel caravan was just going out; we could see the long swaying string, and hear the grave, deep note of their bells. The dawn, the space, the caravan—this, this was the immemorial beauty of Persia, framed for us in the square opening, cut so high up in the cliff-like wall of Yezd-i-Khast; but such moments cannot be held arrested. Imperceptibly the sky was growing more luminous; everything was lulled but the bells; the very silence in which the colours of the sky changed, spread, and became molten, seemed to prophesy some imminent and tremendous event, some royal coming, which should be accomplished only in the hush of a waiting world. He came, tipping the hills with gold, sending a long wave of light rolling over the plain; at first only a rim creeping up above the peaks, but irradiating the whole sky as with a sudden burst of trumpets; then the entire resplendent disc climbing

with unbelievable rapidity: the chariot and the horses
of the sun.

Sitting in the garden at Isfahan I lived again through
the dawn of Yezd-i-Khast with such intensity, that I
really believed myself to be there.   Coming back with
a start, I drifted off again, and stood at the Koran Gate
above Shiraz, looking down on the mosques and
cypresses of the city which lay in a haze of smoke and
sunset.   So that was Shiraz " which turns aside the
heart of the wanderer from his native land "; a long-
dreamed-of pilgrimage, at last I had achieved it.   That
was Shiraz of which Herbert had said with more
picturesqueness than accuracy, " Here art magick
was first hatched; here Nimrod for some time lived;
here Cyrus, the most excellent of heathen princes, was
born, and here (all but his head, which was sent to
Pisigard) entombed.   Here the great Macedonian
glutted his avarice and Bacchism.   Here the first
Sibylla sung of our Saviour's incarnation.   Here the
Magi are thought to have set out towards Bethlehem,
and here a series of two hundred kings swayed their
sceptres."   But it was the soft Persia of the poets;
the Persia of gardens, lutes, and nightingales; not the
austere Persia of mountain and desert that I so loved.
" The black-eyed beauties of Kashmir and the Turks
of Samarcand," said Hafiz, " sing and dance to the
strains of Hafiz of Shiraz "; and even more engag-
ingly, " when thou passest by our tomb, seek a blessing,
for it shall become a place of pilgrimage for the
libertines of all the world."   Maybe.   But what I
remembered of Shiraz was an old man sitting in the

bazaars, carding a heap of snow-white wool; a shaft
of light fell on him; the string of his implement
twanged incessantly; needing not to watch his work,
he looked at us with indifferent inscrutable eyes, so
identified with his craft that it seemed the only thing
which kept him here on earth.

IV

IT is now possible, according to Persian standards, to motor from Isfahan to Shalamzar, which lies at the foot of the Bakhtiari mountains, a distance of little over a hundred miles; a matter of eight or nine hours by motor, but several days' journeying by caravan. We were wise enough to send our caravan on in advance, and to avail ourselves of a Ford car and the abominable track across the desert. The Ford made up in garishness for what it lacked in reliability, being gaily decorated with bunches of yellow and magenta flowers made of dyed feathers, stuck into the hood and windscreen. Lurching from village to village, delayed by many a puncture, we spent a day on that part of the journey, before the road became impracticable even for a motor on caterpillar wheels. Two roads I knew already, leading out of Isfahan to north and south, the Teheran road and the Shiraz road; but this road to Shalamzar, which indeed was scarcely a road at all, was new to me. It rambled through the country in an intimate way; it could not in any sense be regarded as a main road. The Teheran—Shiraz road was unfrequented enough to satisfy most tastes, but still it was a main road crossing Persia, and as such was not sufficiently remote to satisfy my geographical romanticism. I know, somewhere in my heart, that I want to be where no white man has ever been before, far from any place that has ever been heard of. The globe is too small and too well mapped, and the cinema too active.

Our way took us at first through country which was, for Persia, surprisingly well worked and populous. Everywhere the peasants were ploughing between the foot-hills, and a string of villages accompanied us, brown in the midst of their green willows and poplars. A characteristic feature of these villages was the pigeon-tower, round and crenellated, and splashed white with the ordure of the innumerable pigeons; the storks were nesting too, and their large untidy nests straddled perilously on the roofs and at the angles of mud-walls. We stopped for luncheon in the village of Mubaraq, spreading our rugs on the floor of a carpenter's shop in a large barn-like building, among the litter of carpenter's tools and half-made wooden ploughs, the clean smell of fresh-cut wood mingling with the scent of the fruit-blossom that floated in through an open door. The carpenter, a dignified man with his beard dyed a bright orange, had been cutting out, we noted, wooden rosettes exactly similar in design to those carved in stone on the lintels of Persepolis. We had set a servant to ensure our privacy from the curiosity of the villagers, but looking through that open door on to the little walled-in garden we saw that we were not unobserved, for three women, in their black draperies, like the Three Fates, had climbed on to the housetop and were peeping at us from behind their veils. We could not grudge them their entertainment, for it was surely not every day that Europeans passed through Mubaraq; and indeed those three black figures on the housetop, against the sky, made a group which we were as pleased to contemplate as they were pleased to contemplate us. We would have been glad to linger in the carpenter's shop, but as we could not tell what delays might be before us in the shape of broken springs or burst tyres, we reluctantly set off again for Shalamzar.

Very soon we had left the villages and the agriculture behind, and were on the desolate uplands where the only sign of human life was an occasional shepherd, a solitary figure leaning on a long stick while his flock strayed and browsed. These plains would in the summer months be covered with the flocks of the Bakhtiari, but the Bakhtiari had not yet arrived; they were on their way, as we knew, coming up the Road down which we were to travel; they were concentrating on the far-off, unknown plain of Malamir in the south, and we should meet them flowing up, in an endless narrow stream, to these higher, cooler plains of Chahar Mahal. Our frequent punctures,—for the stones were sharp—gave us an opportunity for walking about and enjoying the freedom of these high, airy spaces at our leisure. The love of Persia filled my heart again, at the sight of her high solitudes in the purity of the April day. I rejoiced, as always, in this empty, unfurnished landscape, where the imagination had room to move about, without stumbling over a multitude of objects, beautiful perhaps, but ready-made.

At Shalamzar we were to be the guests of Morteza Khuli Khan Bakhtiari, the son of Samsam-es-Saltaneh, but as he himself was away in Teheran we were received with great ceremony by his steward. Shalamzar proved to be a large country-house in a valley, standing in an oasis of poplar trees, whose young green, very delicate against the snow mountains, gave us a promise of the coming spring. The courtyard was full of movement, for our caravan had arrived—fourteen strong mules with three or four muleteers, plus our escort of three guards,—and for the first time we heard that tinkle of mule bells which was to become so familiar a sound in our ears. Most of the house was shut up in the absence of the owner, but our own camp furniture had been set up in the ground-floor rooms. Presently the steward came to ask if we would not like to go up to the roof. We followed him up to the roof, and stood there looking at the great barrier of mountains flushing pink in the sunset, the track that we must follow being just discernible as it zigzagged up the mountain-side to the summit.

The women of the establishment were weaving in their own quarters. We went to visit them, for the Bakhtiari women have no objection to being seen unveiled. I was sorry that they no longer wore the old Bakhtiari dress which Layard describes—the loose trousers, the white shirt open to the waist, leaving the breast bare, the velvet jacket embroidered with gold, the chin-straps composed of gold coins that jangle like harness. I had seen Bakhtiari women in Teheran, wearing the old dresses, but I knew that they had put

them on for my special benefit, and that they no longer
formed part of everyday life.   These women at Shalamzar were copying an old Bakhtiari silk carpet, the most
beautiful carpet I had seen anywhere in the whole of
Persia.   It was as complete within itself as a lyric
poem,—perfect in design and colour; they pulled it
out of its corner to display it to us, and, a real work
of art, a real unity, it sprang to our eyes in its perfection out of the squalor of the women's room, amongst
the looms and cradles and rags, a perfect thing, in the
satisfying limitation of its rectangular shape.

V

THE time was at hand for us to make a closer acquaintance with our caravan, which on the following morning we found drawn up in the courtyard, jingling, tossing, and loaded, ready to start. Apart from the pack-mules, there were the saddle-mules for us to ride, large raw-boned animals whose sensitive ears I regarded with mistrust. We had three servants between us: Sultan Ali, who was to act as our cook; Rahim, who was to prove the one unfortunate member of the party; and Bagh'er, who belonged to Harold Nicolson, and whose name, unless very carefully pronounced, had been apt to arouse horror and dismay among members of the British colony in Teheran. Besides these, we had three guards: old Hossein, whose chirpings of encouragement behind my mule drove me nearly to distraction; a man on foot, whose name we never discovered; and Taha, who alone came up to our ideas of what a Bakhtiari guard should look like. Taha was dark and spare, on his feet he wore a pair of patent-leather boots, he was dressed in a long black coat with silver buttons, he rode a slim, wild-looking pony, and he carried a rifle slung across his shoulders. This rifle, as we presently discovered, was more for

31

ornament than for use, since the trigger had jammed
and no amount of danger could have induced it
to fire. It was, moreover, repaired on the stock—
or perhaps decorated, rather than repaired—with a
shining tin plate, of which Taha was evidently proud,
but which bore, to our amusement, the words " Keating's Powder ". Keating's Powder, not gunpowder;
that was the pathos of Taha's rifle.

Our escort not inspiring us with much confidence,
our trust reposed in a letter from the Khans in Teheran,
threatening vengeance on the whole Bakhtiari people,
should any harm befall us. This letter, which was
brought to us at Shalamzar by Mirza Khan, Governor
of Deh Kurd and representative of the Persian Government in the Chahar Mahal, concluded with the words:
" If you do not show every courtesy and grant every
facility to the above-mentioned noble persons, it will
be extremely bad for you ".

The morning was grey and stormy, and the hospitable steward seemed reluctant to let us go, for he
assured us that we should be " blown off the top ",
but we took our leave of him nevertheless, and with
our long poles in our hands, like pilgrims, set off
across the valley, followed by our caravan trailing out
behind us, the bells jingling, on this light-hearted
expedition which was to take us down the Bakhtiari
Road. Very soon we got our first taste of climbing;
for we rose from the valley and were on our way up
the Zirreh Pass. Two hours of stiff climbing lifted
us to an altitude of 10,000 feet, and as we paused for
rest at the top, lashed and cut by an icy wind that met

us like a demon on the crest, we saw for the first time
the wild, tumbled Bakhtiari country lying below us
and rising again in new ranges as far as the eye could
reach. The climb had been severe, but the sense of
conquest was exhilarating. Looking back, we took
our farewell of Shalamzar far below, and leaving the
saddle-back of the *col*, plunged down the steep path
among the boulders to the further valley.

Still we could not feel that we were really embarked,
for at Naghan, our first stopping place, we were again
the guests of the Khans in an empty house, and as yet
we had neither seen our tents nor unloaded our camp-
kitchen. By our muscles, however, we were made
aware that the first stage of our journey lay behind us,
and not before. How they ached! It was not so
much the actual miles that we had in our legs, as the
steepness and roughness of the going. I speak for
myself, for the others were in better training; but I
foolishly had set out on feet softened by life in Teheran,
and not only were my muscles, at the end of that first
day, aching so that every step was pain, and weak as
stretched elastic, but my heels were blistered and my
toes bruised; let whoever knows the discomfort of
walking along an ordinary country road with a blistered
heel, try scrambling down a long mountain-side over
sharp stones, and then say what he thinks about it.
But there was no turning back; I reflected with dismay
that days and days of tramping lay before me, not being
then in a fit state of mind to realise that sooner or later
muscles would harden and feet become inured.

VI

I THINK the next stage, from Naghan to Do-Pulan, was the most miserable of all. I really shrink from recalling it. The start was not so bad; we walked along an easy valley, cheered by the sight of the brilliant blue and orange bee-eaters who were flying up in scores from the south, and for some time we sat very happily by the waters of the Ab-i-Sabz-i-Kuh, waiting to be overtaken by the caravan, which, as it turned out, had forded the river lower down and gone another way. Those were the enjoyable moments, when we felt ourselves to be free in the wilds of Persia, and could rest and talk, or look idly round for flowers. When we realised that the caravan had eluded us, we rose to our feet again and walked up the long but gradual pass, which, at the top, pitched down suddenly into a wooded hillside track even more sheer than the drop after the Zirreh. There was only one encouraging sign ahead, and that was the roofs of the village of Do-Pulan (Two Bridges) lying half hidden in the trees at the very bottom of the hill, some three thousand feet below. They looked a long way off; but there they were, and there our camp would be, with food to eat and a bed to sleep on. I freely confess that it was with tears in my eyes—for I really was suffering considerable pain—and in a shocking temper that I slipped and slithered down that purgatory of a path to Do-Pulan. But what a blow awaited us at the bottom! The camp was nowhere in sight, and on making enquiries of the villagers we learnt that the caravan had gone on to a place beyond the bridge. What cared we that now for the first time we saw the green waters of the great Karoun, foaming, a mere mountain stream near the place of its birth, through a narrow gorge of black rock? All we cared about was that we must drag ourselves another two miles to reach our now visible tents. Another two miles, when we had felt that another two steps were an impossibility. Could we but have leapt the river, we should have reached the camp in a few hundred yards, but the bridge was some way down-stream, and we must double back, after crossing it, on our tracks. Those two miles were the longest I ever knew. The bridge, when we came to it, was a crazy affair, put together with a lot of poles, like a drawing by Heath Robinson, spanning the jade-green water between the glistening black rocks. I had just enough energy left to take a photograph. As we stumbled into camp, I found a further reserve of energy. "Why on earth," I said to Copley Amory, who had ridden on ahead with the caravan, "didn't you make them pitch the tents by the village instead of coming all this way?" The accusation was unjust, and I knew it: Copley Amory could speak no word of Persian, and the muleteers, even when addressed in their own language, were as obstinate as their own mules; but I was tired and more than footsore. Copley Amory, being gentle and full of perception by nature, made no retort. He simply spread out a rug for me on the ground. Within five minutes we were all asleep.

We awoke sufficiently restored to turn a still rather indifferent glance on the beauties of nature. Our tents were pitched in an orchard,—on young wheat, as we now observed;—beyond the river huddled the brown village, overhung by the high, wooded hill. Our eyes had adapted themselves so quickly to the mountainous landscape that we should have been surprised to see a flat expanse. We already took it for granted that the world went up and down. But we were not allowed much time to admire our surroundings, for the local *ked-khoda* (headman) arrived, supported by two or three friends, to demand compensation for the damage we were doing to the wheat. Had we paid the sum he asked for, we should have given enough to feed the whole of Do-Pulan throughout the year. The Persians are a good-humoured people, however, and a compromise was soon arrived at. Moreover, the letter which Mirza Khan had given us at Shalamzar went a long way towards pacifying the *ked-khoda's* feelings. This difficulty arranged, we turned once more to our peaceful contemplation and to the ordering of our canvas-sheltered life.

Those who have never dwelt in tents have no idea either of the charm or of the discomfort of a nomadic existence. The charm is purely romantic, and consequently very soon proves to be fallacious. You imagine that you are independent, and can stop the mule by a hiss or an ejaculation in any spot that takes your fancy, but you will soon find that a number of considerations come into play: water, for instance, is more important than you had ever conceived it to be in a country where "company's water" is carried in a convenient pipe-line to most villages. Lose yourself in the mountains of Asia, however, and you will find that a spring or a stream is a more urgent necessity than ideal scenery. Fuel, too: the nights are cold, and the blaze of a fire is a luxury not to be despised. A day or two will suffice to bring you down to the level of the practical. Then as for the discomfort of tents,—a chapter might be written on that subject. In civilised life, we take tables for granted,—tables, flat surfaces on which one may put things down. But in tent life there are no tables. We, journeying down the Bakhtiari Road, had one table, our dinner table, a rickety collapsible thing, on which plates and glasses were precariously balanced; a communal thing, everybody's property. In the tents, those private and personal retreats, there was no room for such luxuries. If you wanted to set anything down, even for a moment, and if it was not a thing which could be hitched to a nail driven into the tent-pole, it must be set down on the bed or on the ground. The bed was the thing you wanted to get into with the least possible delay, and were therefore reluctant to clutter up with heavy or angular objects; the ground was usually wet and muddy; besides, in the Bakhtiari country it was not advisable to put things on the ground, since pilfering

hands were liable to steal under the tent flaps during
the night in search of whatever they might find.
Rawlinson records the Bakhtiari as being most dex-
terous and notorious thieves, and relates the theft of
a horse, " out of a stable in an inner court, which was
particularly watched, and padlocked, moreover, with a
chain for security, that unless I had witnessed I could
not possibly have believed ". This meant that clothes,
cameras and luggage must be piled in the centre of the
tent, out of reach, taking their chance of the damp.
Nothing could be left outside, for the same reason.
Saddles, water-bottles, guns, stores,—all were pitched
recklessly into our tents in the last desperate effort to
get to bed and obtain what sleep we could before the
all-too early dawn came with its signal that we must be
stirring. Nothing could have bred a greater familiarity,
a greater loathing, or a greater affection for our few
essential possessions. We learnt a lot: we learnt how
many things may be discarded; a few days more, and
we should certainly have been sleeping in our clothes.

Barbara, however, was always unpacked. Barbara
saw more of the Bakhtiari country, in the end, than
did our sponges. Barbara was in the happy position
of being inevitably unpacked, since she travelled rolled
up in my sleeping-bag, and that was a thing I could
never have dispensed with. To get at it Barbara had
to come out. Barbara stood every night on the ground
against my tent-pole, leaning her wooden cheek on her
wooden hand as though she suffered from perennial
toothache. Much-travelled Barbara! no Spanish saint,
surely, was ever taken into places so far removed from

the original altar. Harold Nicolson had bought her for a few pesetas in Madrid, and from that moment until the present day, when she has travelled to Berlin, described in the Army and Navy Stores' packer's list as " figure of lady, worm-eaten ", she has never known rest. The period of the war was spent by Barbara in a cellar in Constantinople. After a few years of respite at home she travelled out to Persia in my hold-all, seeing Egypt on the way, Delhi and Baghdad. In Teheran she knew the proudest moment of her life, when a Persian dealer caught sight of her on my writing-table, lost his head, and offered me two thousand tomans for her. Two thousand tomans! five hundred pounds! for Barbara whose marketable value in London might be thirty shillings at the outside. He was accustomed to disinterred amphorae of the period of Darius, but a mediaeval Spanish saint had never yet come his way. I badly wanted the five hundred pounds, but does one barter one's Lares and Penates? Could I betray Barbara, and risk the curse she would surely put upon me? I smiled and shook my head: Barbara was not for sale.

So here she was, riding on a mule all day, and standing beside the tent-pole all night in the melancholy attitude to which she was eternally condemned. It was a humble position that she occupied on the ground, and it was fortunate that she took up but little room, for a small tent is no place for superfluous objects. Our great sheep-skin coats, reeking of fleece and leather, especially when they were wet, were bulky and unwieldy, but the nights were so cold that in spite of them we often shivered. One encumbrance, indeed, we left behind at Do-Pulan: the huge jeroboam of wine which we had brought so carefully up from Shiraz, fell and was smashed to pieces. This was a blow: henceforth, however tired, we should have nothing in the evenings to revive us.

Do-Pulan, indeed, was an unlucky place. Copley Amory's servant Rahim was kicked off his mule and fell on a rock, hurting his back; and I lost my temper at breakfast. Not without provocation. We had had an argument at dinner: Gladwyn Jebb had suggested that we might get up at five in the morning; I went on strike and said nothing would induce me to get up before five-thirty. The sun did not rise till five-thirty; nor would I. My rage, therefore, knew no bounds when next morning Bagh'er entered my tent with hot water at half-past four. It was pitch dark, and bitterly cold, for we were at an altitude of nearly five thousand feet; there was, however, no object to be gained by trying to go to sleep again when the camp echoed with the noises attendant on packing up; besides, I wanted Gladwyn's blood with the least possible delay. A cold grey light had begun to spread over the camp as I emerged, and the last stars were paling in the sky. I fell on Gladwyn with fury, unappeased even when he established his innocence. I recognise, looking back on it, that I must in those first days have proved an extremely disagreeable companion. I suppose I was over-tired.

Those camp breakfasts, when nobody was quarrelsome, had their charm. We ate huge bowls of *mast—*

the native curdled milk, like Devonshire cream,—with spoonfuls of apricot jam stirred into it, making golden streaks in the white. All around us the business of packing up the camp was going on. Tents fell, helplessly collapsing as the pegs were withdrawn, turning from shapely brown shelters to flattened crumpled squares. Our luggage strewed the ground. The blackened ring of our fire looked as melancholy and meaningless as the glasses of a previous night's debauch. Diversions occurred: a mule would kick up its heels as the girths were being tightened, and breaking loose, would gallop through the camp, scattering the contents of its pack as it went, pursued by the muleteers. We ourselves ate our breakfasts as the Jews the Passover: standing, for our solitary chair and the suitcases which were our seats at dinner had already been hoisted up and corded on to the mules. The servants hovered round, ready to snatch away a spoon or a cup to pack it, the moment we set it down. Meanwhile the sun struck suddenly on the crest of a neighbouring hill, and, sweeping grandly down the flank, crept towards us till the light like a low golden tide lapped round our feet. Day had come, and we must be off.

VII

I HAD wanted to walk all the way; my intention had been not to ride an inch—an unproclaimed intention, since I knew that my prospective companions would say, " Then you can't go at all," and there would be no end of a bother and argument,—but after that second day I recognised my defeat. Spiritual defeats have their interest; but this was a mere physical defeat, a shabby affair—simply a question of bruised toes and blistered heels. I should have to climb on to the back of a four-footed animal and allow myself to be transported, a mere package; I who had stalked so proud. A shred of vanity, of self-defence, however, remained: I refused to ride the animal that had been provided for me. Such are the subtleties of the curious process known as " saving one's face ". I felt that, by being tiresome, I had saved my face. No mule would content me but Hossein's special pet, the smallest, most mouse-coloured of the caravan, a pampered creature, to whom a load, other than human, was an unknown indignity; a lazy little beast, to whom kicking, rearing, or running away, even falling over a precipice, would, I instinctively felt, be too great an effort; a mount, in fact, after my own heart, if a mount

I must have.   I remembered how Stevenson had hated
Modestine,—or had thought he hated her, until the
moment came for them to part;—there was no insult
too great for him to heap on that poor beast, and indeed
I suspect him of definite unkindness: did he not bring
her in at the end of the journey " unfit to travel "? and
although he appreciated her quakerish elegance he
admits that his heart remained cold as a potato, nor is
he moved to pity on seeing drops of blood appear on
her small rump under the prickings of his goad.   Now
it was not in me to hate the Mouse, compelled though
I was to ride upon her.   It was not, after all, the
Mouse's fault that my endurance had given out; she
was there, not to humiliate me, but to relieve my
weariness, small, passive, obliging, so that I very soon
conceived a great affection for her and began to talk
of bringing her back to England, a suggestion received with horror by those who foresaw that on
them would fall the burden of making the necessary
arrangements.

The Mouse had this great advantage, that she stood
perfectly still while one climbed on and off, unlike a
horse, who walks away with his rider still hopping
with one foot in the stirrup.   I soon discovered that
by copying the ejaculation of the muleteers I could
bring her to a dead stop, so dead that nothing but a
kick in the ribs would move her on again.   The truth
is that she was always half asleep, except when she had
to choose her way over a bad bit of road, and then she
collected her wits; her long floppy ears would stiffen,
she would pause deliberately to take a good look;

then, having once made up her mind, she would carry
out her scheme with primness and certainty, putting
down her little hooves between the stones with never
a false step, and it must be said in justice to her that
her judgement was infallible; the Mouse never made a
mistake.   She knew exactly what she could do and
what she could not; unlike Taha's horse, who would
stupidly attempt any obstacle his master put him at,
with the result that he sometimes came clattering
down; not so the Mouse, who if she mistrusted her
own powers, after investigation, would turn aside and
go round another way.

Our first ride together took us up a particularly
rough bit of the road, the Barreh Murdeh (Dead
Lamb) Pass, where the track practically ceased to
exist, and lost itself in the rocks that strewed the hillside under the dwarf oaks.   We simply scrambled
over these stones as best we might, bent only on getting
to the top.   We were overtaken by a merchant riding
on a beautiful dapple-grey horse; he waved to us
gaily as he passed, followed by his servant, who, perched
on the top of a pile of carpets on a mule, had some
difficulty in keeping up with his master.

It was cold and the sky looked stormy ahead; we
were not happy; presently a cold small rain began to
fall; the rocks ceased abruptly, and we were making
our way, very high up and still rising, over greasy red
mud; then, as we came to the top of the hill, the rain
changed to snow.   We stumbled along, on foot, in
the teeth of a blizzard, the coats of our mules getting
shaggy with lumps of ice, and our saddles turning

dark with the wet, but it was impossible to ride. We knew that we still had a long way to go; the view in front of us was by now entirely obscured; we were trying to disguise from one another how dreary we thought the prospect, when to our grateful surprise we came suddenly on a hut by the side of the road.

These huts, common enough in the rest of Persia, were practically non-existent in the Bakhtiari country— we cannot have passed more than two or three on the whole length of the road—so our delight was un-bounded on coming at such a moment on this oppor-tune shelter. We crowded in, stamping about, and shaking the snow from our hats, and there was our merchant with his acolyte, squatting on a carpet over the fire. Acquaintance soon ripens between travellers on those lonely hills, and we greeted one another as old friends, for all that our previous glimpse of him had been but a wave of the hand and a shout as he passed us so gallantly beneath the oaks. With the universal courtesy of Persians, he immediately began unrolling his bundle for our accommodation; this bundle contained his bedding; he would not listen to our protests that we were dripping wet, as was all too obviously the case, but spread his quilt and mattress on the floor, inviting us to seat ourselves, which we did without further ado. It was, indeed, almost impossible to remain standing, for the smoke from the fire got into our eyes and made us cry, to the amusement of the Persians, who can sit all day in a hut filled with smoke without the smallest discomfort, but to us it was agony, and even when sitting on the floor at the fire-level, we were constantly obliged to get up and go to the fresh air to relieve our streaming eyes.

At one art the Persians are adept: they can make a fire burn; that is to say, they lay their wood scientifically, in cross-pieces, with a hole for the draught scooped in the embers beneath, which is more than can be said for any English housemaid. So they had a good fire burning, which soon set our wet clothes on to steam; they brought us tea in the usual little glasses; we ate our hard-boiled eggs and our chocolate, talked to our friend the merchant, and felt the warmth running again through our thawing limbs. Still, a long way lay before us, and the snow fell as thickly as ever; we were anxious to start off as soon as possible, lest all sign of the track be covered up. So when the jingle of bells announced the approach of the rest of our caravan, we knew that the time had come for us to take up our sticks, sling the rein over our wrists, and be going. The caravan came up and halted, with drenched packs and heads held down against the driving snow; we allowed them time for the muleteers to shake the snow off their cloaks, to warm themselves a little, rubbing their raw hands and squeezing the frozen drops off their moustaches, to drink a glass of tea and exchange some questions and answers with the hut-keepers about the road; then, taking leave of our friend the merchant, we set off in a long string, blundering over half-covered rocks, sliding suddenly on hidden mud, unable to see more than a short way ahead of us by reason of the falling snow. For a long time we went, advancing perhaps twenty yards at a spurt, then stopping to let the pack-mules rest, which they did gratefully, poor beasts, with heaving flanks steaming on the grey air; and which we did gratefully too, for the going was heavy through snow and mud, uphill mostly, stepping in each other's tracks, punting ourselves along with our tall sticks. It sounds unpleasant; it *was* unpleasant; but for some reason we did not mind much, it was at any rate a definite hardship, and so easier to bear than the poor drab, dragged-out fatigue of the two previous days. In fact, we were quite gay and good-humoured, and ready to laugh when anybody fell down.

Sultan Ali, the cook, that Napoleonic man, was the only one who took it wrongly. He was not accustomed to snow, and, like a camel, could not deal with it at all. I came on him sitting on a boulder, nursing his toes, almost in tears. Apparently he had heard of frost-bite, and thought that this calamity had overtaken him. He was of course wearing the white canvas shoe which is the Persian's national foot-gear, and was soaked to the skin; but when I pointed out to him that such peasants as we had met were walking barefoot, carrying their shoes in their hand, a sense of shame goaded him and he revived enough to stagger on. "Why not ride?" I suggested, but he looked at the mules, most of whom were fallen and floundering under their packs in the snow, and mournfully shook his head. I could not but sympathise. A bedraggled Mouse followed me; I had no inclination to ride myself.

Then we came to the inevitable descent, which always seemed the hardest part, at the end of a long day; and zigzagged down the rough track to the village of Gandom Kar. It was amazing to me that the mules could keep their feet, under their heavy burdens. Yet they got down without mishap, and we came down upon the two or three houses which constituted the village, and again dried ourselves in a hospitable hut, while the population looked on, interested but never importunate, and a girl fed her baby meanwhile at her young brown breast.

VIII

I REMEMBERED the gardener at Isfahan, who had told me that *Iris reticulata*, that gold-and-purple early comer, grew at Gandom Kar, so when we had eaten I went out to look for it. *Iris reticulata* was nowhere to be seen, needless to say; but the hills were blue with grape hyacinths, among the young corn, glistening with drops of rain, and narcissus (not in flower) grew in large patches in swampy ground; still, I was disappointed at not finding *reticulata*, having meant to collect at least a thousand bulbs.

There is a peculiar pleasure in bringing home plants which one has collected oneself in distant countries. Quite possibly that pleasure may plunge its roots in the fertile soil of vanity; " Yes," I should say, " a nice group, isn't it? I collected the bulbs in the Bakhtiari country." But that would only be when strangers were present, forced to admire my garden. Indeed, so rathe is *Iris reticulata*, that they would scarcely be able to find anything else to admire. But on February evenings, when I strolled alone, the oaks still bare in the woods and the rooks busy after the plough, surely it would be a purer pleasure that I should get from the gold-and-purple patch springing out of the wintry ground? Or is vanity so deeply rooted as to be still operative even *vis-à-vis* oneself? Would the sight of the little iris, the little alien, which may be bought from any nurseryman, but which had been brought by me from its native hills, awaken in me merely the satisfactory reflection that I had not always been, after all, an armchair traveller? Would a feeling of superiority rise in me, that none of my friends had ever been to Gandom Kar? Honesty compels me to admit that such is probably the case. I have a pan of rhizomes, which throw up a feeble green shoot in spring, indicating that some faint, terrified life survives in them, and I know in my secret heart that I printed the wooden label not entirely for purposes of identification; no, for even without that label I should remember well enough what that grit-filled pan contained. Yet I printed, " IRISES—QUERY, SMALL BLACK? FROM THE PLAIN OF PASAGARDAE—TOMB OF CYRUS—APRIL 1927." It is true that no one sees it, for it stands on cinders in a secluded corner with suitable companions—" SPECIE TULIP, YELLOW, FROM THE JARJARUD HILLS "; " ROSA PERSICA, QUERY, ORANGE? " " IRIS, SMALL BLUE—FROM SHIRAZ "—but there is always the offchance that some true botanist might stray that way, and incline his head obliquely to read the labels. And then I should feel—quite unjustifiably—enrolled in the company of Reginald Farrar and Kingdon Ward.

Iris reticulata at Gandom Kar certainly deprived me of that satisfaction. Authorities on irises give it as a native of the Caucasus, and ascribe to it in its wild state a reddish-purple colour different from the blue-purple it displays in English gardens. But the *reticulata* I saw in flower at Isfahan were undoubtedly blue-purple, and the gardener was positive that they came from Gandom Kar in the Bakhtiari country. I offer this to iris experts without comment. The villagers, to whom I appealed, and who in their charming Persian way were at once eager and interested, denied, although regretfully, all knowledge of the flower. " Nerkis! " they said at once, meaning narcissus; but I was not looking for the narcissus. (I have, however, flowered the Persian narcissus without any difficulty in England; it has a very sweet and slightly different scent.) The grape hyacinths were not worth bringing home, for, unlike the Italian variety, they were entirely without scent. Besides, they were of an inky blue, almost black; attractive only through the great profusion in which they grew, as thick in the young corn as bluebells in an English wood. Disgusted with the failure of my search, I returned to camp, only to find that Gladwyn Jebb, who had gone out to look for partridges, had come home, not with partridges, but with a bunch of Crown Imperials. This revived my hopes, which, excited by Mrs. Isabella Bishop's accounts of the " innumerable flowers ", had been sinking slowly as we progressed day by day, finding nothing on our path but a few mauve crocuses and a small though brilliant scarlet ranunculus. Mrs. Bishop, however, was writing of May and June, and I fancy that her carpets of tulip, iris, primula, and blue linum had not yet made their appearance in April.

We stuck the Crown Imperials into the ropes of our brown tents, and the camp looked more festive than we had seen it since we started. Our spirits rose accordingly. We lit a huge fire and dined beside it, in the content which comes of physical fatigue when not too excessive, and which is begotten of the sense of having overcome a good day's difficulty. A Bakhtiari in a white cloak galloped past on a white horse as we dined; seen in the glow of our fire, in the dusk, his white cloak floating out behind him, he looked ghostly and romantic; a visitant out of the hills. Our camp was pitched on a long natural terrace; we looked towards the south, down a gorge where a river tumbled; the sky was stormy, and thunder rolled intermittently among the hills, but nothing interrupted our night's rest except the barking of a dog and the conversation of our guards as they sat round the fire.

IX

Next day we plunged down into the gorge, following
the river by a ledge of path.   Harold Nicolson and I
were alone with Hossein, the others having, more
prudently, as it turned out, remained behind with the
caravan.   At this low level, shut in as we were by the
high cliffs of the ravine, the temperature softened with
every mile; the air became warm and steamy; the
stunted oaks, which up on the Barreh Murdeh Pass
had been bare, now burst into leaf; dripping rocks
overhung the way, sprouting with fern and mosses; the
coarse green leaf of autumn crocuses covered the banks,
and Crown Imperials, stiff as the flowers on a Gothic
tapestry, shot up, brilliantly orange, between the
boulders. (We noticed, however, that a large proportion of the bulbs came up "blind", as is their dis-
appointing habit in English gardens.)   In all this long
ravine we met nobody, but had it all to ourselves, with
the rush of water and the narrow strip of sky overhead;
we could not see or hear even our own caravan, which,
as we afterwards discovered, had taken another path
and so missed out the gorge altogether.   Now the
road bent downwards, and led us across the river, into
the thick wood of oak that grew on the opposite bank.

It was dark in there, and the track disappeared; we had to make our way, bent double to escape the branches, slipping and sliding in greasy black mud on a sharply tilted slope. We met a peasant who, recognising perhaps that we were in distress and in need of consolation, gravely offered us some sticks of wild celery. Up till then, Harold Nicolson and I had very carefully avoided making any comments to one another about our journey, but now our tacit resolution broke down. " This damned country! " we said, almost in tears, " why did we ever come ?" We agreed that we did not even think the scenery beautiful. " I *loathe* mountains," he said, standing there in the wood, muddied up to the knees. " I *hate* tents," said I. " We've got to go on with it, though," we said. We stared at each other, so woebegone that we finally burst out laughing.

The grumble improved our spirits, and we ploughed our way out of the ravine, till we came to a place where we could ride, and climbed another hill, all alive with hoopoes and the cuckoo. It had not occurred to us that we had, in fact, lost our way, so that we were puzzled by the manifest anger of Taha when he rejoined us at a canter, coming from the opposite direction. It was in the same state of defiant innocence that we met the others safely with the caravan, in the village of Gumish-Su. Where on earth had we been? they wanted to know, irritable as people are irritated with relief after anxiety. Blandly we described the beauties of the ravine they had not seen. Crossly they retaliated that we, by our impetuous foolishness, had missed Sarkhun, where an ice-cold river joins a warm underground river issuing from among the rocks. Defiant and aggrieved respectively, we ate our sandwiches in no very amicable mood by the stream at Gumish-Su, and a sarcastic note which will be found in the appendix at the end of this volume testifies to the displeasure we incurred from Gladwyn Jebb.

A heavy rain began to fall and we sheltered for some time in the chai-khaneh. Harold Nicolson, who characteristically had forgotten to bring a coat, bought for a few *krans* a cloak of stiff black felt from a peasant; as the sleeves, which were half the usual length, were sewn up into a point and stuck out like stumps on either side, it made him look like a penguin, but at least it kept him dry. Thus equipped, we set out again, and after a long ride up another muddy pass, came out on to a level of high country showing us a new burst of mountain ranges, with a beautiful distant view of the snow-covered and rounded peak of the Sabzeh Kuh. It was muddy all the way, however, and we began again to curse and despair, not knowing that that was to be our last day of serious mud, and that henceforth we should be on rocky tracks, which, however painful to the feet, were preferable to this slime. The sight of our friendly merchant, once more overtaking us in his gallant way on his fine horse, cheered us for a moment. But the way seemed very long indeed that day, and my temper grew correspondingly short. I could gladly have pushed poor Taha over a precipice, rifle and all, when in answer to my enquiries he could only reply: "Nasdiké, nasdiké,—quite near, quite

near." It was useless to ask, " How far? " for Taha's
reply would have been given in *farsakhs*, and the
Persian *farsakh* is by no means an exact measure of
distance, but varies according to the nature of the road;
that is to say, a *farsakh* of uphill going, or over a stony
road, is longer than a *farsakh* downhill or on a smooth
road. Roughly speaking, it means the distance that a
mule or horse can cover at a walking-pace in an hour.
With my previous experience, I felt pretty sure that
before we could be " quite near " we should have to
go down another of those long zigzagging descents,
stubbing our toes against the stones, and sure enough
we presently came to it and pitched rapidly down into
another gorge, with another foaming river, the Bazuft,
fondly hoping that at any moment we might see the
welcome sight of the grazing mules and the four brown
tents. The camp was nowhere to be discovered.
" Nasdiké, nasdiké," said Taha, making a gesture of
encouragement. We went along the path, which led
up and down, up and down, in a maddening switchback
above the river, now climbing up the hilly bank, now
swooping down again till it brought us nearly to the
water's edge, but never by any chance on the level.
The gorge was certainly a fine one, had we not been
too tired and cross to care.

X

WE found our camp, finally, pitched within the broken walls of the ruined caravanserai of Shalil. The muleteers tried to persuade us into one of the rooms of the building, which they said was warm; warm it certainly was, but it was also thick with smoke. We preferred to shiver in our tents, after tramping down the lacy hemlock which grew waist-high, as though it were still in the open air with no dwelling of man, however transitory, roofing it over.

Scarcely had we settled in, and collected enough wood for a fire, than a messenger arrived accompanied by a large black sheep. He was the bearer of an invitation from some Khans encamped a few miles down the road. Would we not pack up our tents, and consider ourselves their guests for the night? They were preparing a *pasirayi*, or reception, in our honour. Appalled by the prospect of packing up our tents, and knowing only too well how Persian receptions were apt to be prolonged, we decided to risk offending our hospitable though unknown friends, and despatched the messenger with a polite refusal. The sheep remained behind with us, and we ate it for our dinner, reminded thereby that Omar appreciated the value of mutton, for in that quatrain which is familiar in its more poetic English rendering he says:

> " If a loaf of wheaten bread be forthcoming,
>   A gourd of wine, *and a thigh-bone of mutton*,
>   And then, if thou and I be sitting in the wilderness,
>   That were a joy not within the power of any Sultan."

The next day dawned warm and sunny. It was almost the first time we had seen the sun, and certainly the first time we had felt any heat in it. Shalil in the early morning light was very lovely; the river rushed musically down the valley, and the hillside opposite, where the sun was striking, was sprinkled with moving flocks. Our path led us along the valley; it was no gorge like the gorge below Gandom Kar on the previous day, but a fairly wide and gentle valley, with well-wooded slopes; in no way dramatic, but pleasant enough, though we could not help slightly resenting this tame scenery, having travelled so far to find it. " We might as well ", we said, " have gone to the Tyrol." But there was plenty in store for us that day which we should certainly not have found anywhere but in the Bakhtiari hills.

The path, soaring upwards, brought us out on to the hilltop. Here we met a fine young man, riding on a fine horse, and attended by a servant. He galloped up to us, pulling his horse almost on to its haunches, to greet us in the most friendly fashion. This was Nosratollah Khan, the son of Sardar Zaffar, the Il-Khani; in his long white robe, with his rifle slung across his shoulders and his black eyes flashing as he

smiled, he cut a very handsome figure among his
native hills. The Khans were awaiting us, he said;
and inwardly groaning, since we were not to escape
the *pasirayi* after all, we took leave of Nosratollah and
pursued our way. It was not long before we came
upon the nomads' camp. The black tents were pitched
on a ledge overhanging the river Bazuft, which cut its
jade-green way through a narrow gorge of rock hundreds of feet below. Why they had chosen that dizzy
place for their encampment we could not imagine,
unless they liked a grand view, or were actually happier
perched on a ledge in constant danger of rolling down
the slope. Anyhow, there they were, and came out to
meet us, leading us in through the squalor of the
servants' quarters, to a tent which had been got ready
for the *pasirayi*. There were cushions and carpets, and
trays of little sweets, and of course tea and cigarettes.
Conversation was not difficult, for the Khans were
naturally eager for news of the outer world, and we
for our part had plenty of questions to ask about the
road. But if the conversation was not difficult, it was
long. We began to grow anxious, for we had a long
way to go, and the sun was already high, but the
Khans showed no disposition to speed us on our
way, and to the Persian mind it is not only rude
but incomprehensible to be in a hurry. Besides,
our principal host, Ali Khan, for all his courtesy to
us, appeared to be in an irritable mood, swearing
at his servants, and we did not want to offend him.
Had it not been for our anxiety about the time, it
would have been pleasant to sit there in the tent,

watching the remarkable scene which was taking place before us.

For there, on the steep hillside, rising from the opposite bank of the river, we beheld for the first time the tribes really on the move. So far, we had met but few people on the road: our merchant with his carpets, the Il-Khani's son, a stray herdsman or a group of charcoal-burners, a solitary caravan coming up with petrol from the south. But henceforth, as we could see, we should be engulfed among the nomads. We had as yet very little idea of what this would mean; we saw, indeed, the slope covered with moving figures, but we scarcely realised then that those figures represented but the advance guard of a stream which would flow against us even until we reached Malamir.

We must, we said finally and firmly, be going. At that, Ali Khan gave an order, and a little brown lamb was brought in, with a brass bowl ready to catch the blood from its throat. We begged, however, that the lamb might be spared, though what we really meant was that we ourselves should be spared that horrid sight, and that it might be allowed to accompany us alive. Our hosts were amused at this, but acquiesced at once, and rose to escort us out of the camp. The cause of Ali Khan's irritability then transpired. He was not, he said, feeling very well: could the English, who were all doctors, do anything for him? Lionel Smith extracted his medicine chest from the pack of a mule, and stuck the thermometer under Ali's tongue. The other Khans all crowded round to watch. Lionel Smith then examined the thermometer, but seeing that he looked very much puzzled we enquired what was the matter. He said he couldn't find the mercury, for which he was looking in the region of 100° or 101°. We all peered into the thermometer in turn, and discovered that he had been unable to find the mercury because it was up at the other end of the tube: Ali Khan, in fact, had a temperature of 108°. Fearful lest the man should die before our eyes, and we be blamed, we left him a large supply of quinine and hastily took our departure.

We were told afterwards that men frequently run such temperatures in the mountains, but continue to go about as though nothing were the matter. Poor Ali Khan, no wonder he was irritable.

XI

Down at the foot of the hill, in the gorge where the bright-green river crept between the rocks, we halted and looked up at the hill we had to climb. The whole hillside was noisy with bleatings. It seemed, as we gazed upwards at the trail, that the hillside was in fact coming down upon us; as though the stones and boulders had been loosened, and leapt down the hill, now singly, now in a moving flood, pouring down steadily from the very summit, with incessant cries among the stunted oaks. Far overhead, in the blue, planed a couple of eagles. The morning sun blazed still in the east, throwing long blue shadows on the distant snow-mountains. And the air was filled with the distressful cries of the flock as they poured down the precipitous slopes, driven onward by the voice of the shepherds.

Twice a year, in spring and autumn, the tribes move. In spring they go up from the scorched plains towards which we ourselves were travelling, to the higher plains of Chahar Mahal; in the autumn they come down again, driving all their possessions before them, over the two hundred miles of the road. And here were we in the midst of them,—very literally in the midst, for the flocks surged round our mules, making progress impossible, and we had to sit patient in the saddle, looking down upon the sea of backs, till the way was cleared and the mules were able to scramble a few yards further, up the steep rocky track, with a sudden straining of the muscles, a sudden putting forth of strength; and when we stopped again, the green river below us seemed a little further away, the beat of the sun a little more powerful. We were going against all that moving life, being always confronted with faces and never with tails, driving our wedge into the stream, that parted for an instant and then closed up again and went on; it gave one, more than anything, the sense of slavery, of necessity; these nomads, I thought as I kicked the Mouse into another scramble, for all their independence are not really independent at all; they are hunted and driven, they all go the same way, like the rest of mankind; and we ourselves felt pleasantly exalted by the flattery of travelling in the opposite direction.

So many thousand faces. The long, silly faces of sheep, the satyric faces of goats with their little black horns; the patient faces of tiny donkeys, picking their way under their heavy loads; and then, six or eight little heads of newly born kids, bobbing about, sewn up in a sack on a donkey's back. For there were a great number of kids and lambs; in fact, a great deal of young life of all sorts. The older ones were obliged to run, skipping over the stones, kids and foals and calves and children, but the youngest had to be carried: a litter of puppies slithering about on a

mule's pack, a baby in a cradle slung across its mother's
shoulders.   The hens travelled too, perched on the
back of a donkey.   Behind each separate herd—for
each herd, in its way, represented a self - contained
little family—came the men, beating the stragglers
up with sticks and uttering strange cries which the
beasts recognise and obey; then came the women,
also beating up the stragglers, young women in bright
red and yellow shawls, old women who must have
crossed the mountains a hundred times.   They were
all too weary or too apathetic to stare much at us.
Some, indeed, stopped us to make a practical enquiry:
was the snow deep on the passes? were the rivers in
flood? was the mud bad? for we had come down the
way they must go up, and in those hills news circulates
only by word of mouth.   We reassured them; they
nodded dully, and passed on.

We had come down the way that they must go up,
and knew the exhaustion that lay before them, the
passes to be climbed, the steep descents that would
lead them down on the other side, the changes of
weather, the long stretches up the ravines where the
greasy mud checks every footstep.   But for us, each
difficulty conquered was conquered for ever and left
behind; we should not pass that way again.   For
them it was different.   It was only one journey among
many journeys, renewed twice a year from the cradle
to the grave.

In complexion they were swarthy, with tufts of
black hair curling out from under the *kolah*.   The
blue linen of their long coats emphasised the natural

darkness of their skin. The men were all clean-shaven, and rather high cheek-boned; the broad Tartar type was common. Some of the younger women looked handsome as they passed us on their lean ponies, their heads covered by their gaudy handkerchiefs; but it was clear that the hard life aged them prematurely, and their bodies, moreover, were hunched and shapeless under the ragbag of garments in which they were clothed. They sat on their ponies, merely an extra bundle piled on the top of the other bundles.

The Bakhtiari are a proud people: they claim that they alone, among the Persians, remained unconquered by Alexander. This is a double boast, vaunting alike their warlike spirit and their ancient origin. To this day they are quarrelsome and independent, settling their disputes according to their own code, dealing out violent justice to their own transgressors, resentful of governmental interference. They choose their own leaders, the Il-Khani and the Il-begi, although they do, in fact, acknowledge the suzerainty of the Shah; but the Shah is in Teheran, and Teheran is a long way off. But the casual traveller down the Bakhtiari Road would not be predominantly impressed either with the proud savagery or the idyllic simplicity of this people. Rather, he would bear away the sense of the weariness of a pastoral cycle; the sense of necessity in the struggle for mere existence. Those who have seen it, know that the beauty of a pastoral life is largely a literary convention. The truth is that nature is as hard a taskmaster as civilisation, and that realities under such conditions are very bare facts indeed.

The men who drive the flocks are tired. The women who follow the men are tired too; often they have just become, or are on the point of becoming, mothers. The children who drag along after their parents limp and whimper. To us, who come from Europe, there is something poetic in a Persian shepherd calling to his goats and sheep; but the Persian shepherd himself sees nothing except the everyday business of getting a lot of tiresome animals along. Since romance is the reality of somewhere else or of some other period, here, on the Bakhtiari Road, this truth is doubly applicable. Persia is certainly somewhere else, and a long way, too, in relation to England, and this Biblical form of existence certainly belongs to a period other than the twentieth century—it is an anachronism in our eyes, and therefore romantic; the double elements of space and time, geographical and chronological, necessary to romance, are thus amply satisfied. We are on the Bakhtiari Road, in one of the wildest parts of Persia; let us accept it at its face value, and see what is to be got out of it in terms of the picturesque. Let us be quite cynical about it; let us, by all means, be romantic while we may.

The hillside, then, is alive with flocks. " Baa-a-a! " go the sheep, and " Meh-h-h! " go the goats. They bleat, they bleat; even to-day, in England, when a flock of sheep is turned loose into the meadow at the bottom of my garden, and their bleatings reach me, I whirl back to the Murvarid Pass, and feel the sun hot on my hands; a queer sensation, analogous to that sensation with which one wakes at night convinced that one's bed has turned itself round the other way. There are thousands of them, jostling, leaping, hustling each other among the boulders. Some of them are very lame, but what of that? That is reality, not romance; lame or not lame, they must go forward. There are two hundred miles to cover before the sun gets too hot and the already scant pasture shrivels up. So the shepherds come after them with sticks. " Oh ", say the shepherds,—a flat, English " Oh " that sounds curiously out of place on the Persian hills. Oh. A real Cockney vowel. But the beasts respond. They leap forward as if in terror. We, on our mules, sit motionless while they huddle by. The men take very little notice of us, unless they stop to ask a question; they do not seem to notice that we are Europeans,— and, as such, figures of romance to them, surely, coming as we do from another place? No, to them we are simply a caravan travelling in the opposite direction, an obstacle, albeit a patient and long-suffering obstacle, to be passed. Oh. And the sea of backs surges round the legs of our mules. The smell of fleeces comes up to us, acrid. The men follow, in their blue linen coats and high black felt hats, and their sticks fall with a thud on the woolly backs. Oh. The sun is hot and high. The jade-green river flickers in the sun down in the ravine. The snow-mountains stretch out like a spine in the distance. An old woman passes us on foot, carrying across her shoulders a limp baby donkey.

Some squawking, flapping hens pass, perched on a load of pots and pans on a pony's back. A litter of puppies, that presently will be savage, camp-guarding dogs, but now are round, woolly, and frightened, pass clinging and sliding on another pack. They try to growl as they go by, but without much conviction. A child passes, beating up his flock of lambs and kids,—youth put in charge of youth. Oh. And then a fresh shower of sheep and goats, animated boulders. How stony the road is! How slow our progression! Come along, come along. Oh.

This, then, was life shorn of all mechanical ingenuity. One forgets too readily that there are still places in the world which civilisation has been utterly unable to touch. Even the wheel, most elementary of mechanical devices, here did not, could not, exist. Dawn, the hour at which one started; dusk, the hour at which one stopped; springs, at which one drank; beasts of burden, to which one bound one's moving home; a beast from the flock, which one slaughtered and ate fresh; fire; a story; sleep. There was nothing else.

In the evenings we saw the nomads under a different aspect, when we had pitched our own camp, squatting by their black tents, the smoke of their pipes rising upwards with the smoke of their fires, while the women cooked and the animals strayed browsing. It was then, when they were at rest, and the sense of their weary progress was suspended, that the charm of a pastoral existence reasserted itself. Along the road, one was conscious only of harshness, violence, and fatigue. The

limping horse, the dying ram, the woman near to her
delivery, the man with his foot bound up in bloody
rags—all these were painful sights, made more painful
by the knowledge that there could be no respite and no
relief. But in the evenings, in some quiet valley, with
a spring gushing from a rock near by, and the moon
newly risen from behind the hill, then the world did
indeed seem to have returned to an early, limpid
simplicity. Theocritus and the Bible took on a fresh
and more vivid significance. The pastoral and the
patriarchal, ceasing to be decorative merely as a convention of literature, became desirable also as a part
of life.

Meanwhile we climbed for most of that day,
conquering step by step the Murvarid Pass, only to
drop down again, having reached the top; and as
evening fell we came down on the lovely valley of
Deh Diz, with its single sentinel poplar and a ruined
castle in the distance, and the long ridge of the snowy
Kuh-i-Mangasht beyond. Our camping-place this
time was in an orchard of pomegranates, beside a clear
mountain stream, on a grassy terrace strewn with rocks
and boulders. The ropes had already been untied; the
packs had fallen to the ground; the men were bending
over them sorting out our possessions; the little brown
lamb which the Khans had given us, and which had
trotted meekly all day beside our caravan, was hanging
dead and skinned from a bough with a drop of blood
at the end of its nose; a thread of blue smoke was
already rising from our kitchen. The evening was very
soft and serene, the surrounding hills enormous and

shadowy. A sense of peace crept over our weary limbs, and a sense of sudden intimacy with this quiet spot, which none of us, almost certainly, would ever see again. Already its contours were familiar, and someone had picked a handful of the little wild pink gladiolus, and put it in a glass on our rickety camp table. It is curious how quickly, in this kind of life, any resting place becomes home. It is as though the mind, instinctively rejecting the implication of transitoriness, sought, by an excessive adaptability, for compensation. Yet we knew that when we left at daybreak on the following morning, no trace would remain of our passage but the blackened ring of our dead camp fire and four squares of trodden grass, that were the floor of our tents. The golden oriole will return to the myrtle bough, and the spring will bubble without any memory of those who stooped to fill their cups.

XII

But we were not destined to leave Deh Diz on the
following morning. As we were sitting round the fire
after dinner, we heard a distant clap of thunder, and
the muleteers came running up to say that a storm
was upon us. From the minutes between a flash of
lightning and the next clap, we reckoned that we had
twenty minutes in which to prepare. Everybody ran
in different directions, some to knock the picket-pegs
of the mules firmer into the ground, others to perform
the same office for the tent-ropes, others to dig little
trenches round the tents, others to carry our dinner
table into shelter. Scarcely were we ready for the
storm when it burst upon us. We five had all gathered
together into the biggest tent, and as the storm crashed
above us we hung on to the tent-pole with our united
strength, expecting every moment to be carried away,
tent and all, in the sudden gale of wind that tore
screaming up the valley. The hail came down in
torrents, battering on the canvas, and we thought
thankfully of our little hastily dug trenches. Peeping
through the flap, we could see the valley wholly
illuminated by the magnificent flashes, with which the
thunder was now continuous; the snow on the distant

71

ranges gleamed white, and the valley showed an unearthly green, as the sky was torn asunder as with a swift and golden sword. The storm swept on; we heard it cracking over the hills; it was as though the wheels of a great chariot had driven over us, in the heavens, and were now rolling onwards, above the oak forests and the black tents of the crouching nomads, describing great circles, and returning now and then to visit our camp at intervals through the night.

XIII

WHEN we looked out in the morning, we saw to our astonishment that the ground was white with snow. There was no chance of continuing our journey that day: the mules could never have carried the weight of the soaking tents. We were condemned to a day of inactivity at Deh Diz. By ten o'clock, however, a warm sun had melted all the snow and the tents were steaming like the flanks of a horse. We hung all the wet things we could find on the tent-ropes to dry, and stretched ourselves on rugs in the sun, to the delight of a circle of inquisitive villagers. It was a change to spend such a lazy day. We read the Apocrypha, I remember, and wandered a little, but not very far afield, not much further than the spring where we refilled our water bottles; we admired the village giant, a grand figure at least seven foot high; we talked with a wandering dervish, who strayed up to our camp carrying a sort of sceptre, surmounted by the extended hand of Ali in shining brass; we listened to a blind man chanting an interminable poem about hazrat-i-'ísá (his Majesty Jesus) ; we watched the procession of women going to the spring. They crept past, with their empty goat-skins, stealing furtive glances at us out of their long dark eyes; then scurried on, in a burst of mischievous giggling, like a lot of children caught in a conspiracy. Presently they returned in a more sober mood, weighted down by the heavy, black, dripping goat-skins that lay shining across their shoulders and drenched their blue rags. We watched them, as one watches shy animals creeping out of a wood,—the wood of their secret, unrevealed lives, spent in the mud-houses of Deh Diz, among bickerings and jealousies and hardships, crouched over a pot on a smoking fire, to the upraised voice of the mother-in-law, and the cry of the child, till the figure of a man darkened the entrance, and a babble arose, and a clutching for the partridges he carried in his hand. Very secretive they looked, as cunning as slaves and as silly as children, but pretty under their snoods of blue, with the characteristic surreptitious walk of those who go barefooted under heavy burdens. So we idled, becoming acquainted with the habits of village life in Deh Diz, while our mules wandered loose among the pomegranates, cropping at the grass, and the eagles circled high over the hills where the gladiolus and the gentian grew.

XIV

THE stage between Deh Diz and Qaleh Madresseh lay through the most beautiful country we had as yet seen. We were now in the very heart of the ranges. The road after first leaving Deh Diz is rather dull; it follows the valley, in a switchback of small descents and small ascents, wearisome and monotonous. We had to find our interest where best we could,—in immediate anticipation of the future, and distant memorials of the past,—that is, in a man ploughing with two bullocks amongst a scatter of boulders, yelling and groaning at his beasts, as his primitive plough jerked up and down the slope, turning the sod which perhaps would grow him a handful of corn in autumn, perhaps, and perhaps not,—in a wayside cemetery, where among blood-red poppies stone lions of archaic design commemorated the valour of bygone Bakhtiari. Poignant little cemeteries, these, lost in the hills. Lions used to abound in these mountains, and the Bakhtiari, when they did not want to fight the lion, had a special code for dealing with him. Lions were of two kinds, they said : Moslems and infidels. They might be known by their colour, the Moslem having a bright yellow coat, the infidel a darker coat, with a black mane. On meeting the Moslem it was sufficient to say, " O cat of Ali, I am the servant of Ali ", when the lion would retire into the mountains. On meeting the infidel, however, the wisest course was to take to your heels.

Lions are reported even to-day in the Pusht-i-Kuh, the range stretching to the north-west of the Bakhtiari range, and bears are known to exist still in the Bakhtiari country; and leopards, notably the snow-leopard, but we never saw so much as the spoor of any such animal. Wolves, lynxes, and hyenas were also common in Layard's day, adding to the dangers which that indubitably brave man had to face whenever he set out, sometimes alone, sometimes with a guide whom he justifiably mistrusted, to look for tombs or inscriptions among the unmapped hills and valleys. I thought of Layard often as I rode along. It is easy enough to confront dangers when one is in perfect health, but Layard himself never knew when an attack of ague would not compel him to dismount, and, lying on the ground with his horse's bridle fastened to his wrist, spend two or three hours in delirium and unconsciousness. An unpleasant predicament, in a country infested by murderers, marauders, and wild animals. A brave man, I thought, as I looked at the stone lions among the poppies.

By midday, we had rejoined the Karoun, and were riding along a rocky path sheer above the river, which presently brought us to the splendid gorge of Pul-i-Godar. Here the Karoun winds between pointed hills, to lose itself again in the intricacy of the ranges.

We left it far below us, for after Pul-i-Godar the track rose steeply, bringing us to the top of a pass, with truly splendid views over the tumbled country. Strange geological convulsions had heaved up the hills; the strata, which were as definitely marked as though they had been gigantic slates laid flat one against the other, stood up on end instead of lying horizontally superimposed; in some of the hills the lines of strata were actually vertical, in others they were aslant, so that one could imagine one saw the huge processes still at work. In the course of ages, those masses of rock would shift under the weight of some unseen pressure; that which was now oblique would become perpendicular, and that which was now perpendicular would gradually heel over until it slanted to the opposite side. These mountains were being slowly turned upside down. It was not so much the grandeur of the landscape which impressed one—though that was sublime enough—as the awful evidence of nature labouring on a cosmic scale. The wild loneliness of the place, the ramifications of the valleys leading up into unknown fastnesses, the track made by generations of men crossing the mountains—all this produced a sense of some elemental strength which excited and yet sobered the imagination.

And now came the tribes, the slow-moving, inevitable tribes, winding up through the hills in a long and constant stream. Dwarfed though they were by their native scenery, dwarfed into crawling battalions along the narrow ledges, they still seemed an integral part of the country. It seemed right that these mountains should witness their pilgrimage in the two temperate seasons, and right also that the mountains should be left to their own loneliness during the violence of summer and the desolation of winter.   On the Murvarid Pass we had met the tribes coming down upon us; now, as we made our way down into the valley towards Qaleh Madrasseh, we met them coming up towards us, their upturned glances swiftly reckoning the best way to pass, their animals struggling up from rock to rock.   Down, down, round the hairpin bends, seeing the path far below, still covered with that moving life; down, right down, into the valley where the black tents were plentifully sprinkled about. Then—rest, on an open grassy space hemmed in by hills; another day was over.

But Rahim, the well-meaning and unfortunate, tripped over a tent-rope and upset our soup.

XV

WHAT would happen to oneself, I wonder, if one were to spend a long time in such a place as Qaleh Madrasseh? A week, a month, a year, thirty years? Thirty years. If one were to go there at the age of thirty, and remain fixed till one was sixty—the most important years of life drifting by at Qaleh Madrasseh? One would explore the paths running up into the mountains, mere goat-tracks; one would come to some unmapped village; one would meet and talk with a number of fresh, ignorant, and unsophisticated people. One would come to know every wild flower in its season, and every change of light. But what would happen inside oneself? That is really the important thing. The only goat-tracks one wants to explore are the goat-tracks of the mind, running up into the mountains; the only sophistication one really wants to escape from is one's own. To start afresh; unprejudiced; untaught. Changes of light, coming from the internal illumination, not from the play of limelight over a ready-set scene. Away from papers, away from talk (though not, I stipulate, wholly away from books); cast back on personal resources, personal and private enjoyments.

Thirty years at Qaleh Madrasseh.

Of what is civilised life composed?   Of movement, news, emotions, conflict, and doubt.   I think these headings may be expanded to fit every individual requirement ?   Now at Qaleh Madrasseh most of them would be deleted: movement certainly, except such slow and contemplative movement as could be performed on one's own legs; news certainly, except such local and practical news as would brush one in passing by word of mouth.   But what of the growth of the mind?   The mind would have only its own rich pasture to browse upon.   It would rise superior even to these tribes flowing backwards and forwards,—and in the space of thirty years it would witness the flowing of the tide sixty times;—it would be filled with the sense of its own inexhaustible riches, dependent upon no season, dependent upon no change of pasture from Malamir to Chahar Mahal, no exchanging of the south for the north.   The mind would browse and brood; sow and reap.   Few of us have known such leisure. Those who achieve it are called eccentrics for their pains: it seems to me that they are among the wise ones of the earth.   The world is too much with us, late and soon; we are too stringily entangled in our network of obligations and relationships.

Those who crave for and find their fulfilments in action would not be satisfied.   But I write as one with a strong head for large draughts of solitude.   In fact, I suspect that I should look out for some less frequented spot than Qaleh Madrasseh, some place further back in the mountains where I should not see the tribes go

by. To live encamped even within sight of the
Bakhtiari Road, that rude, violent, and occasional
highway, would more than satisfy the misanthropy of
most people. It would not satisfy mine. To me,
remote places hold the magic which the romantic
names held for Marlowe or Milton. (It is my only
justification for writing books of travel.) The analogy
is exact save in this particular: Marlowe had never
seen Persepolis, but I have; Milton had never seen
Trebizond, but I have seen Qaleh Madrasseh. Therefore I have my feet more firmly on the ground than
either Marlowe or Milton. I know what I am talking
about; to me Qaleh Madrasseh is reality, to Milton
Trebizond was only a means of escape. Ithaca, Fiji,
would have served his purpose as well; as to the
Bakhtiari shepherd, shouting " Oh ! " at his goats,
Grasmere. One name is as good as another, provided
it be sufficiently unfamiliar. Proust himself, for all
his caustic intelligence, was not proof against the
romantic appeal of proper names. Not only did the
names Guermantes, Saint Loup, Cambremer, evoke
for him the romance of a world which he affected to
deride but by which he was obviously fascinated;
but Proust himself, taking flight for once from Paris,
shows that he could be allured by the exotic no
less than Milton and Marlowe. " On serait venu
pour me voir, pour me nommer roi," he says, " pour
me saisir, pour m'arrêter, que je me serais laissé
faire, sans dire un mot, sans rouvrir les yeux, comme
ces gens atteints du plus haut degré du mal de mer
et qui, en· traversant la mer Caspienne, n'esquissent

même pas une résistance si on leur dit qu'on va les
jeter à la mer." The key of the sentence lies of course
in the words " mer Caspienne ". Proust uses them
as Milton or Marlowe would have used them, with the
only difference that neither Milton nor Marlowe would
have associated the Caspian Sea with so realistic a
probability as sea-sickness. But I, when I say Qaleh
Madrasseh, mean Qaleh Madrasseh. I mean that
exact spot, whose contours I have learnt, whose clefts
I have contemplated, enviously, running up into the
mountains and had no leisure to explore. So far, at
least, I am on solid ground. But of the effect of
solitude in such a place I know no more than did
Marlowe or Milton. That is a speculation which, no
doubt, would never have occurred to either of those
great poets or to their humbler contemporaries; they
had not acquired the habit of playing with hypothetical
complications as we have acquired it. The very
mention of the name sufficed, Persepolis and Parthia,
Ternate and Tidore, to hang an agreeably rosy veil
between themselves and reality; it brushed an Orient
glow across their pages; they felt no need to follow up
the implications to their logical conclusion. Had anyone suggested their visiting Parthia or Persepolis,
Tidore or Ternate, they would no doubt have recoiled
in dismay. For one thing, they probably had but a
very vague idea of where these places were situated.
But I protest that, did occasion offer, I would eagerly
embrace those thirty years at Qaleh Madrasseh, though
with an equally vague idea of what the consequences
might be. What, for instance, would become of one's

capacity for emotion? would it become stultified through disuse, or sharpened through denial? What would become of one's power for thought? Would that become blunted, in the absence of any whetstone whereon to grind itself? Or would a new, high wisdom arise, out of an inhuman sense of proportion, accomplishing nothing and desirous of no achievement, but attaining through contemplation a serene and perfectly tolerant estimate of the frailties of mankind? For one would arrive at Qaleh Madrasseh, at the beginning of the thirty years' seclusion, not as an Oriental mystic, having no experience of the world of intellect, vanity, and science, but as a fully equipped exile from a European state in the agonies of its striving after civilisation. Glutted and weary with information, confused with creeds, the old words knocking against one another in the brain and producing no more than a tinny clatter, one would settle down either to a stagnant repose or else to a concentrated readjustment of values.

The very idea of stagnant repose being execrable, one repudiates it without further consideration. Thus one is left exiled at Qaleh Madrasseh with an army of facts waiting to be drilled into order. Facts,—that incongruous assortment which accumulates,—snippets of knowledge, fragments of observation, fleeting theories no sooner formed than discarded, ideas as self-contradictory as proverbs—at last one would have time to marshal all this into some sort of formation. An army indeed; and every unit as complicated as the soldier himself, as intricate and capable of as many interpretations. Personal conceit, however, suggests that one would deal successfully with the matter; so successfully that at the end of the thirty years one would emerge upon the world crying with a voice as the voice of a prophet.

A whole flock of reflections arises, as suddenly as a flock of starlings from the ground. But although I should like to go into the question of exactly what form one's proselytising would take—whether he who had once had leisure to open his own mind would burn with the desire that his fellows should do likewise; whether it would be, not evil, but stupidity, that he would attack; reason, and not faith, that he would demand,—I feel that this is no place in which to do it. A minor and more frivolous question comes uppermost: society. Because, of course, at Qaleh Madrasseh, society as we understand it would be entirely absent; and society is the recreation upon which the enormous majority of people depend. Mankind is, in fact, gregarious. Now the craving for society takes many forms, from Mr. and Mrs. Humphrey Turnbull, who, with Miss Aminta Turnbull, arrive at 157 Pont Street (telephone Sloane 0673) at the most exquisite moment of the year " for the season ", down to Mrs. Godden, who, after she has given the potato parings to the pig, goes to a whist-drive in the village. The most curious thing about all such activities is that the participants enter into them as though at any moment something truly exciting were liable to happen. From the Turnbulls' point of view, this optimism is justifiable: Aminta may meet an eligible young man who will marry her, and a new household will be set up which will then start off revolving in the approved cycle. But this can only be said of anxious couples with marriageable daughters. It cannot be said of those who go yearly through the same routine; and who would probably admit, were the habit of hypocrisy not so firmly taught them from their youth upward, that the dominant impression was one of boredom and monotony. Conversation is different, and the meeting together of intimate friends; but what conversation does anyone get at a party? And who would not rather meet his intimate friends elsewhere? The fact remains, that mankind is gregarious. Probably we do not realise to what an extent most of us are dependent upon contact with our fellows; we do not realise it until we contemplate in detail such a severance as would result from living at Qaleh Madrasseh. We are, in fact, seldom alone; even if we avoid parties, we are probably in such constant contact with a little group of familiars that it is difficult to disentangle their ideas from our own. We are, indeed, seldom alone. We are a patchwork quilt of colours. The pressure of other minds is enough to pulverise our own. Even if we are of a taciturn habit, the printed word still remains to rape our singleness.

But at Qaleh Madrasseh?

What luxuries, what relaxations, would one allow oneself? A yearly post, including one copy of the *Times*? The newsagent would obey orders, but one's friends, would they write? They might write in the first year, even in the second, but after that? One would, I fear, soon become as unreal, as remote, as a distant catastrophe, and one's image would evoke little more concern than an earthquake in Japan. A passing irritation, a flush of impatience at such extravagant eccentricity,—idle to hope for more. It would be, even with the best will in the world, difficult to write to a person once a year; it is easy enough to write every day, but in a yearly letter the writer would feel, inevitably though mistakenly, that only dramatic and portentous news was fit to put on paper. The power of imagination would quickly dwindle; no correspondent could reasonably be expected to realise the drawing near of the awaited day, say the 23rd of September, or to visualise the arrival of the messenger with his pouch. He would be late, probably; the post-cart would have dawdled on its way down to Isfahan; his mule would have gone lame in the mountains; he himself would have been prostrated with fever. Day by day, for a week, for a fortnight, after the appointed date, one would have gone down to the Road, and with hand-shaded eyes stared at the track,—in vain. The 23rd of September; it would be hot then in the Bakhtiari hills, the tribes would still be up at Chahar Mahal; the long empty months of summer would have dragged by; no one would be travelling the Road, so that any figure sighted in the distance would be, could be, none other than the awaited messenger. Homesickness, absent from the eleven uneventful months of the year, would rear its head, and with scorching breath burn and devastate the savannahs of calm. At length the messenger would come,—but let us pursue the matter no further,—it is too painful to contemplate,—or let each one fill in the story for himself as he will.

A wireless set one might have, a super-set that would pick up London. I remember that an Englishman condemned to live in a little malarial town in Persia told me that he, having come into possession of such a set, arranged with the only other Englishman living in the town to meet and listen to Big Ben. At one o'clock in the morning they sat together, and listened to Big Ben striking ten. They belonged to the usual inarticulate type of Englishman, and it was in silence that they parted, but with tears upon their cheeks. I like to imagine that one would sit alone at Qaleh Madrasseh, listening, as the dead might listen, to London. Then, I fancy, it would be one's childhood and adolescence that one would try to revive. Modernity would make no appeal; the too obvious homesickness and sensuality of syncopation would leave one unmoved. Nothing but the eternally sublime or the sentimental associations of vanished years would twang the chords of the heart. Beethoven's Symphonies and the Ode to the West Wind; Daisy, Daisy, and the Bicycle made for Two; there would, I fancy, be no middle stage. And that, again, would be part of the ceaseless endeavour to escape; as much a part of it as the voluntary exile to Qaleh Madrasseh.

Perhaps it would be better to go the whole hog and cut oneself off entirely from the outside world. A merely negative form of protest, I fear, against conditions one does not like; for resentment is vain unless one has an alternative to offer. Flight is no alternative;

it is only a personal solution. But as a personal experiment it certainly offers material for reflection to the curious.

The story is told, indeed, of an Englishman who in the beginning of the last century settled down among the Bakhtiari, took to himself a wife, and spent many years living with the nomads under the name of Dervish Ali. But, " in process of time, having grown tired of savage life and of his Bakhtiari bride, he sold her for a jackass, which he rode to Trebizond, and embarked thence for his native country, having turned a few shillings on the speculation ". This story, entertaining though it is, does not get one very far, except perhaps as a proof that the desire for escape will, after sufficient indulgence, be replaced by the desire for return.[1]

[1] This story is given by Lady Sheil in her *Glimpses of Life and Manners in Persia*. She quotes extracts from the diary of Dervish Ali. Query: can this diary still be in existence?

XVI

I OBSERVE, however, in some dismay, looking back over these pages, that I have given an entirely wrong impression of the Bakhtiari mountains. I have, unintentionally, represented them as over-built and populous; I have mentioned villages; I have mentioned a merchant on his horse, a man ploughing, the son of the Il-Khani, the keepers of a *chai-khaneh*. All this, in the aggregate, must I fear have given the impression of a walking-tour through some part of Europe, with never more than a few niggardly miles intervening between one reminder of civilisation and the next. Nothing could be further from the truth. By the very use of the word village, with its associations in an English mind, I have probably evoked a picture of something much larger, more orderly, and more definite than is justified by the few poor hovels of Naghan or Do-Pulan. For the rest, our path lay along miles of country where not so much as a mud hut was visible. The merchant, the man ploughing, were figures so isolated and so exceptional that I have recorded them as it were greedily, for the sake of having something human to record. They were—let me emphasise it—isolated instances; and, as such, they made an impression on us which in the swarming countries to which we Europeans are accustomed they would not have made. No, the dominant impression was one of isolation. True, we were on the Road; we met an occasional traveller; we met the migrating tribes; but we knew that to the left hand or the right lay utter solitude; the solitude of nature, which draws us and holds us with a primitive, an indefensible attraction, all of us, however sophisticated we may be. And it was a double impression: of isolation and anachronism. Not only had we gone far away in distance; we had also gone far back in time. We had returned, in fact, to antiquity. We were travelling as our ancestors had travelled; not those immediate ancestors who rolled in their coaches between London and Bath, or between Genoa and Rome; but as Marco Polo had travelled, or Ovid going into exile, or the Ten Thousand hoping for the sea. We learnt what the past had been like; and what the world had been like when it was still empty. Time was held up and values altered; a luxury which may be indulged to-day by anyone who travels into the requisite parts of Asia. More: we knew that had we not elected to travel the Bakhtiari Road at that particular time of the year we should not have met even the tribes, but should have had the mountains all to ourselves, eccentric invaders of majestic desolation. No merchant would have overtaken us beneath the oaks, no peasant groaned behind his plough. We should have topped the pass above Deh Diz and seen not only the lonely range of the Kuh-i-Mangasht, but known that in the whole of that valley no human being drew breath. Those whom we did meet were as transient as ourselves; the only permanence was in the hills and in the rivers that coiled about their base.

XVII

NEXT day we were again in the thick of the tribes, riding up the long wooded valley of Cheshmeh Khatoun, very much delayed by the press of beasts and men, as the track here was extremely narrow. The valley of Cheshmeh Khatoun—the Lady's Fountain,—was very shady and beautiful, but it was also sinister. I have said little about the more violent and sinister aspect of the road. A lake of blood by the wayside was no uncommon sight—though whether something had been born there, or whether something had died there, it was impossible to determine. Birth and death fell into much the same perspective: they were just events, the one at the beginning and the other at the end of the same journey. It was curious to note how rapidly the sensibilities of civilisation were modified, in this contact with life reduced to its most elementary forms. We grew so well accustomed to a blood-stained track that we ceased to notice it; and a company of vultures circling and swooping above some nauseating meal stirred us to no interest. Nevertheless I remember still with a shiver of horror and pity the sight of a child, in that very valley of Cheshmeh Khatoun, swaying on a pony in front of its mother, its

head broken open but unbandaged, its teeth chattering
with shock, and a frightened, half-sobbing whimper,
—a pitiful little morsel of humanity.　Wherever we
stopped on the road the sick came to us in a trustful
way that made our ignorance a shame; for consumption, ophthalmia, and syphilis were rife, and although
in most cases we realised that we could do nothing, we
never had the heart to say so, but used to distribute
lint, lotions, and medicines which at least we were sure
could do no harm.　Perhaps the mere suggestion of a
cure, and the abracadabra with which we accompanied
our distribution of remedies,—even though it were but
a pinch of permanganate of potash,—had a salutary
effect on those ignorant minds.　" You know you can
go to the hospitals of the Company ", we said sometimes, "and receive treatment."　But they shook their
heads mournfully: the treatment was good, they knew
that, and the treatment was free, but the Edareh—
the Company—the great Anglo-Persian Oil Company
—was down at Masjid-i-Suleiman, many days' journey
away.　So they took our little packages reverently, as
we ourselves might receive a ring from a magician,
and carried them off, cupped in their hands, like
treasures.　We alone were left with the burden of the
knowledge that it was no infallible talisman we had
given them.

　　On our way up the Valley of the Lady's Fountain
we met a most beautiful girl, decked out in brilliant
colours, leading her horse across a stream.　She and
her horse together looked so wild and beautiful, among
the rocks, with the water splashing round their feet

and the sun falling on them through the overhanging leaves, that I unhitched my camera from the saddle of the Mouse and aimed it in their direction. Whether the young woman thought it a weapon or an instrument of the evil eye, I do not know; but she uttered a piercing scream, dropped the bridle, and fled for her life up the path she had just come down. Her fellow-tribesmen tried to stop her by barring her passage, but she broke through them all in her panic, and leaping up the rocks with goat-like agility,—considering how she was encumbered by her very voluminous clothes,—she came at last to bay, high up on the steep bank, where she clung, gazing down on us in terror, while her fellows roared with laughter and we tried to reassure her with apologetic phrases. Had she but known how beautiful she was, in her coloured plumage, poised as for further flight, her great dark eyes wide with panic, clinging to the rock beside which she had taken refuge, she surely could not have grudged me a whole film of photographs. As it was, I abandoned the attempt, showing her clearly that I was restoring the camera to its case on the Mouse's saddle, but as we rode on up the valley and looked back we saw that she had not yet ventured down from her retreat.

From time to time, riding up this valley, as elsewhere, we came upon stretches of cobbled road. The track would suddenly cease to be a mere beaten way, coiling between the boulders, and would rise for perhaps fifty or a hundred yards in wide shallow steps of hewn stone. The mules took it with relief, and we realised that their hoofs were clicking, as they climbed,

on no less a causeway than the famous Jeddai Atabeg,
the great artery which in the days of the Sassanian
dynasty led from the plains of Susiana to Persepolis.
The squalor of the tribes was suddenly overshadowed
by the might of those tremendous names.   Worn,
discontinuous as they were, those patches of pavement
still represented the reckless and brutal energy which
drove a road across the mountains.   What hands had
laid them there?   The Lurs attribute them to the
Atabegs, the former rulers of Luristan, but Layard
carries the road back to the time of the Kayanian
Kings, and Lord Curzon refers it to Sassanian or even
Achaemanian times.   De Bode, who rode up from
Malamir as far as Qaleh Madrasseh, tries to identify
the Jeddai Atabeg with the Climax Megale or Great
Ladder discovered in the mountains by the soldiers of
Alexander, and quotes Diodorus Siculus and Pliny to
prove his point: " In a province of the interior," says
Pliny, " towards Media, is a place known by a Greek
name, Climax Megale, which is ascended with difficulty and by means of steps, up a steep mountain
leading to a narrow opening through which Persepolis
may be reached, the capital of the kingdom destroyed
by Alexander."   Whether de Bode was right or wrong
—and I believe that he is generally assumed to have
been wrong—mattered little to me who am no anti-
quarian.   What mattered to me was the evidence, the
survival of a grand civilisation pushing its way up into
the mountains of Luristan.   Communication must be
established between Susa and Persepolis; a range of
mountains intervened; no matter,—let a road be made

across the mountains.   The road, one might fancy,
was made by men who in their outward appearance as
in their mental condition differed very little from the
men who were passing us now in their unending
streams.   But among them stood the terrible ghosts
of Shahpur and Ardeshir, Darius and Alexander.

At the head of the valley after the Sarrak Pass, we
came suddenly out on to a wide plain.   This was
much more like the Persia we knew, unlike the Bakhtiari country, which had a character quite its own.
Away from the woods, away from the hills, escaped
suddenly from the valleys, we felt that we breathed
once more a larger air.   For almost the first time, too,
since we had left Shalamzar, our feet were on something flat.   The relief was greater than I could have
believed.   I realised then with what yearning and
affection I had been thinking of smooth, level places
such as station platforms or London pavements, while
the muscles of thighs and calves ached with the per-
petual effort of going up or down hill, over rocky
ground where every step threatened to sprain an ankle;
I realised then how gladly I would have given my soul
for a stretch of concrete, as gladly as the traveller lost
in the desert would give his soul for a drink of water.
The plain was smudged with flocks, and peppered with
little mauve irises.   A few miles in that fresh, clear
air brought us to the edge of the plateau, from where
we looked down upon the wide and lovely plain of
Malamir.   The plain of Malamir is the great gather-
ing-place of the Chahar Lang division of the tribes
before they move off on their march.   Among the

patches of flocks which we could see moving below us were many black tents; and the dome of a shrine, round and white in the sun. We had a long zig-zagging descent before we reached the lower level. It was very green and warm down in the plain. Corn was growing, and camels were grazing; we had not seen a camel since Shalamzar, so now, looking at the long-legged camel foals, straddling and spider-like, we deluded ourselves with the idea that we were out of the true Bakhtiari country for good and all, and might now look forward to the level travelling across plain after plain that we had learnt to expect from Persia. We looked back at the snow mountains, could scarcely believe that we had crossed them, and went forward, the mules stepping sedate and pleased on the short grass.

But it was not only the true Persia that we had seen again as we stood overlooking the plain of Malamir. In the far, far distance, beyond the hills, a dark plume of smoke rose straight into the sky. Taha, reining up his horse, pointed to it as the Israelites to the Promised Land. " Edareh! Edareh! " he exclaimed with almost religious fervour. Edareh—the Company, —the smoke of the oil-fields—civilisation. A wave of regret swept over me; I forgot the exhaustion of our toiling days; I would have turned back then and there to plunge into the mountains again and be lost for ever.

The village of Malamir lay on the other side of the plain, a squalid collection of mud houses with wattled roofs, goats and dogs lying about everywhere in the sun of the main street. Here we stopped to eat a bowl of *mast*, and here it was that I had my second photographic misadventure. It was really very unlucky that I should have had two such misadventures in one day, for, as a rule, the Persians enjoy being photographed, and crowd eagerly, often too eagerly, round a camera.

It was at the end of the street that I came across the dervish. Harold Nicolson and I were strolling alone, the rest of the caravan having gone on in advance. He was a particularly handsome dervish, dressed in a flowing robe of sapphire blue, his heavy black curls descending to his shoulders, and he was mounted bareback on a young chestnut stallion. Riding as he was with the grey amphitheatre of mountains for a background, he presented an exceedingly noble appearance. Mindful, however, of the girl in the valley, I called out to him first to ask if I might take his photograph. He was delighted. He pulled up his horse, sat very erect, and re-arranged his blue robe to show it off at its best possible advantage. I, for my part, put down the camera on the ground, and began to step the distance for the focus. Stepping distance for a focus, as all photographers know, entails taking large steps which will measure a yard each. As I drew near to the dervish, who was already preening himself and affectionately fingering his cavalier love-locks, his young horse, alarmed at my menacing stride, took fright, and after one tremendous plunge which unseated his rider, made off at full gallop, snorting and throwing up clods of turf across the plain. The dervish lay on the ground, his turban in the dust, and his beautiful blue robe billowing round him. As he was an elderly man and had come a heavy cropper, and was now groaning aloud, we rushed up to his prostrate figure, fearing not only that he had broken his limbs but that we ourselves were in immediate danger of being lynched by the villagers. Harold Nicolson especially, who had an ineradicable though demonstrably mistaken view that Persians resented being photographed, was now almost triumphant because, as he thought, my obstinacy was to prove the cause of our being both torn limb from limb. The Persians, however, are a humorous people, to whom the spectacle of a man falling down is quite as funny as to anybody else, and the Bakhtiari, moreover, are apt to think of a man in terms of his horsemanship. Instead of being indignant with the foreigner for thus abasing a holy man, they burst into fits of derisive laughter against the holy man for allowing himself to be unseated from his horse. Some of them set out in good-natured pursuit of the horse, now a mere speck careering across the plain; others propped up the dervish, who with great presence of mind in the midst of his groans had summed up the situation, and was demanding damages for three broken fingers. It seemed cheap at the price. Harold Nicolson, relieved to escape so lightly, turned out his trouser pockets and with a handful of *krans* and *shai* made up a sum of one *toman*—four shillings. This was taken in charge by the friendly villagers, who with broad grins assured us that the dervish had only suffered a shaking; and leaving the sapphire-blue figure still rolling in the dust, we made off in the direction of the distant caravanserai.

We walked on across the plain, emancipated for the first time from the irksome solicitude of Taha or Hossein, and as we walked, Harold Nicolson discoursed hotly on the iniquity of disregarding the prejudices of people in their own country. Abashed by the incident of the dervish, I refrained from pointing out that it was not the holy man but his horse who had objected to my camera. A couple of Bakhtiari, passing us at a wild gallop, put an end to our dispute, and we walked on with friendliness restored, as indeed it could not fail to be in the heart of the warm exquisite evening which was sinking down on us. Even in Persia, I had seldom seen the landscape dyed to more beautiful and subtle colours in the light of the setting sun. The great grey cliffs of rocky strata flushed to rose and lavender, with deep blue shadows in their clefts; a serene immensity seemed to pervade the world, and everything to be at peace.

XVIII

A DISAGREEMENT arose next morning between us and
our muleteers. From notes which we had accumulated
from other travellers we had decided to make for a
place called Murdafil. The muleteers, however, denied
the existence of any such place, and declared, moreover,
that we should find no water except at the place they
wished to go to, called Agha Mihrab. Gladwyn Jebb,
who managed all that part of the expedition with a
calm and haughty efficiency, would have nothing to
do with their arguments. To Murdafil we intended
to go, and to Murdafil consequently we were going.
We set off from Malamir on a hot morning, through
rolling country where the vegetation was far richer
and more interesting than it had been in the hills.
Orchises, iris, anemones, borage, convolvulus, Star of
Bethlehem, gladiolus, eremurus grew everywhere in
great profusion; and on a slope I found to my joy the
little scarlet tulip for which I had looked in vain in
other parts of Persia. The white, starry tulip, and
the yellow tulip had been common, but so far the
scarlet one had eluded me. There it was, blood-red
in the sun, and I took the bulbs, and stuck the flowers
into the harness of the patient Mouse.

As we drew near to the end of our day's march, wondering whether we should indeed find Murdafil or whether we should be compelled to camp in some waterless place, and own ourselves defeated, we came to a sloping valley down which rushed a stream overhung by oleanders and pampas grass. The whole character of the country had altered, and by nothing was it so well indicated as by this complete change in the vegetation, so rich and green that we might almost imagine ourselves in the tropics after the severe aridity we had hitherto associated with Persia. Just above the stream we presently descried the ruins of some small building, where we decided to camp for the night; yes, said the muleteers with smug satisfaction, this was Agha Mihrab, the site they had recommended. We gave up Murdafil with as good a grace as possible, though we were sure they had deliberately and obstinately misled us. There was certainly nothing to complain of in the site: the ruins were raised up on a little natural terrace, in the midst of what had once been a garden, for some old, unpruned rose bushes grew rampant, and down in a dip grew a grove of dark myrtle. Wandering off while the monotonous process of unpacking began, we came on a waterfall that splashed down over a high wall of rock, and here we found a goatherd piping to his goats. What was the name of the ruined caravanserai we had passed some way down the road ? we asked him, and received the reply, Murdafil. We were amused rather than irritated by this characteristic example of the working of the Persian mind; for the muleteers must have known perfectly well that we should find them out in their lie, and that we should establish not only the existence of a place called Murdafil, but also the fact that it lay by a stream of clear mountain water. But when we taxed them with the lie, they only put on a blank expression and shrugged their shoulders.

It was very warm and peaceful at Agha Mihrab. I remember the place with affection and gratitude, as one of those memories which nothing can take away. The note of the goatherd's reedy flute rose above the sound of the waterfall, and mingled with the other sounds of night: the snap of a burnt stick, the tinkle of a mule's bell, the croaking of a thousand frogs down by the stream. We had been sitting in silence round the fire, smoking, while Venus travelled slowly across the sky and now was about to dip behind the hill. I knew that by climbing the hill opposite I could still see Venus for a little longer, in all the splendour of the clear, black night. But I was too tired. Better to let the day go out quietly, when Venus was thus silently extinguished; better to let it go out on the note of the flute, as the red fires burnt low in the valley, and the nomads wrapped themselves in their cloaks and slept.

XIX

"Let us consider, then, what kind of life will be led by the persons thus provided. I presume they will produce corn and wine and clothes and shoes, and build themselves houses; and in summer, no doubt, they will generally work without their coats and shoes, while in winter they will be suitably clothed and shod. And they will live, I suppose, on barley and wheat, baking cakes of the meal and kneading loaves of the flour. And spreading these excellent cakes and loaves upon mats of straw or on clean leaves, and themselves reclining on rude beds of yew or myrtle boughs, they will make merry, themselves and their children, drinking their wine, wearing their garlands, and singing the praises of the gods, enjoying one another's society, and not begetting children beyond their means, through a prudent fear of poverty or war. . . . And thus passing their days in tranquillity and sound health, they will, in all probability, live to an advanced age and, dying, bequeath to their children a life in which their own will be reproduced.

"Upon this Glaucon exclaimed, Why, Socrates, if you were founding a community of swine, this is just the style in which you would feed them up!"

To-morrow, then, was to be our last day of walking? for we knew that the black plume of smoke, although we could not now see it, shut in by the valley as we were, must be drawing ominously nearer. The soft peace of Agha Mihrab made for meditation. Crossing the mountains had been no ordinary or light experience, but it was not enough to record the grandeur of the peaks or even the passing of the tribes: what else had emerged? It was of Persia that I found myself thinking; not, for once, of Persia in her natural

beauty, but of Persia as the ideal state, of the op-
portunities of a wise and idealistic dictator. Would it
not be possible for this vast, majestic, and under-
populated country to shut itself off from the miseries
of the world, and, self-contained, to concentrate solely
upon the well-being of its own inhabitants? That
would indeed be a new venture in government, a bold
and revolutionary programme, which, like all innova-
tions, would call down upon the head of its inaugurator
the bitterest gibes and accusations. " A reactionary
Shah ", one can see the headlines. A triumvirate of
Christ, Napoleon, and Florence Nightingale would
not be too much for the task. But consider: is the
idea really so Utopian? It is first of all essential
to turn all our ideas topsy - turvy, to discard the
principle that excessive wealth, complicated politics,
and facility of movement are necessary to human
happiness, and to exchange for those three fallacies
the ambition of securing Health, Sufficiency, and
Security for all. Geographically speaking, Persia is
not badly situated for a policy of isolation. In its
present railwayless condition, when all journeying
must be accomplished by road, it is for all practical
purposes apt to become inaccessible during the winter
months, when the passes are blocked by snow, and no
one knows what delays and even dangers may not
attend the caravan or the motor convoy. This, save
in so far as it inconveniences the traveller and may,
more seriously, threaten the north of Persia with famine,
matters very little, for Persia does not lie upon the
road to any active or important centre,—nothing but

the darkness of Central Asia stretches beyond it;—consequently the problem of transport becomes merely an internal problem, and one which in the complete absence of mechanical facilities is not likely to concern the outer world.   It is only when Persia talks of building railways that Russia and Great Britain begin to take an interest.   But it will be objected that a sentence or two back occurred the ominous words, "threaten with famine ": that, surely, puts upon the question of transport a different complexion?   And what about trade?

First as to famine,—for it is idle to make Utopian suggestions unless they can be supported in a practical way.   There is no reason why enough crops should not be grown in Persia to supply the whole of the population, if all towns and villages lay in the midst of their own circle of cultivation,—as, to a very large extent, they already do: I quote the highest authority in defence of this contention, the late Administrator-General of Persian finance: " In the areas actually under cultivation at present, production can probably, by obvious and practicable measures, be increased sufficiently to support a population two or three times as great as the present population of the country." The great difficulty at present is the inadequacy of the irrigation; but, although immense tracts of stony and waterless desert stretch between village and village, Persia is by no means a waterless country: the majority of villages are built beside a stream, and moreover water is brought by underground canals from the inexhaustible supply on the mountains, a system of canalisation which, if simplified and extended, could turn each oasis of agriculture into a patch as fertile as the valley of the Nile. As for the meat supply, I have already mentioned the words sheep, goat, and cow so often and so inevitably in these pages that I shall not here insist upon the riches of the pastoral tribes. Which reminds me of the comment of a lady in London sitting behind me at a film taken in Southern Persia. Rugged mountains, sunlit plains, and other beauties of nature on a majestic scale had been displayed before her without arousing any audible response. It was only when she saw a flock of sheep crawling across a plain that she spoke. " Lovely mutton ", she murmured wistfully, " they must have there."

And what about trade? As half the revenue of the country derives from the customs tariff, it is obvious that Persian trade cannot afford to drop below its present figure. Even an ideal state needs a sufficiently furnished purse. Countries are not run upon loving-kindness. But, again discarding conventional and accepted ideas, is there any reason for desiring an increase of commerce? Persia can produce nearly everything she requires for herself, with the exception, of course, of manufactured articles; she is one of the few countries in the world which, owing partly to the simplicity of her needs, can aspire to be self-sufficing. Those who would Westernise Persia naturally take the desirability of factories and machinery for granted, but such an ambition is the negation of everything that this particular ideal state stands for. Granted, says the economist; but money, money is needed nevertheless for the agricultural expansion you have already suggested, and for the various reforms which you are surely about to suggest? I reply that if internal taxation were reorganised and honestly controlled, and trade maintained in its present condition, enough for all my reforms would be forthcoming.

The transport question, then, which occupies so much attention, becomes less weighty if the first principle of my scheme—isolation—be adopted. It reduces itself almost entirely to a question of communications within the country, and for that a solution might be found in two ways: a light goods railway running from, say, Teheran to Bushire, with branches to serve such towns as Yezd and Kirman (Isfahan and Shiraz of course would be served by the main line), or by an organised system of motor-lorries,—these to be merely an amplification of the post-cart system in use already. For I am not so reactionary as to deny that it is more convenient to send a bale of goods by motor than on the back of a camel, or for a man to travel in the same way. On the whole, I incline to the lorries, for the railway might prove to be the thin end of the wedge, and I would risk no wedges driven into the walls of my ideal state. The lorries also would be cheaper to establish, and cheaper to maintain. I sat at Agha Mihrab visualising a blue lorry, ornamented with the Lion and the Sun, drawing up before the mud walls of Dilijan, while plump and clean villagers came out to crowd round it.

But before my villagers could be fattened up and washed, drastic alterations would have to take place in the internal administration. That Augean stable must have, not an irrigation canal, but a cataract poured through it, and over this task our imaginary Shah would be lucky if he escaped with his life. Tradition, national character, and, in Persia, the priests, are stubborn foes to contend with. Many oppressive systems would have to be swept away,—I spare you the details,—and justice and integrity established in their place. Easily said!

Let us assume, however, that this is accomplished, and that we are now presented with a Persia sufficiently and scientifically cultivated, adequately linked together in the matter of internal communications, reasonably taxed, and justly administered. (Smile, you who know Persia!) The wisdom of Christ and the determination of Napoleon have done their work; now it is time for Florence Nightingale. It is idle to feed those peasants or to enable them to travel to the next village if they are riddled with disease. And disease, in that high clean air,—no overcrowding, no factory towns, very little chance or danger of contamination from outside,— should be almost as easy to control in Persia as rabies in England. Why, even the Miana bug might be dealt with. Two things of course are at the root of it all, two things almost (but not quite) as hard to overcome as corruption and the priesthood: dirt and ignorance.

Here, again, national character blocks the way. Call it ignorance, fatalism, or apathy, still the effect is the same. There is a passage in Gertrude Bell's *Persian Pictures* which I shall quote in illustration,

since her authority is higher than mine.   Cholera was
approaching Teheran with rapid strides, " yet, with
the cholera knocking at their doors, they made no
preparations for defence, they organised no hospitals,
they planned no system of relief; cartloads of over-ripe
fruit were still permitted to be brought daily into the
town, and the air was still poisoned by the refuse which
was left to rot in the streets. . . . Another disease
follows on the heels of cholera: typhoid fever is the
inevitable result of an absolute disregard of all sanitary
laws.   The system of burial among the Persians is
beyond expression evil.   They think nothing of washing the bodies of the dead in a stream which subse-
quently runs the length of the village, thereby poisoning
water which is to be used for numberless household
purposes, and in their selection of the graveyard they
will not hesitate to choose the ground lying immediately above a *kanat* which is carrying water to many
gardens and drinking fountains."

There is no need to insist on the truth or fidelity
of this quotation, or to remind travellers of the sights
they have seen in Eastern countries—the eyes clotted
with flies, the festering sores, the swaddled limbs of
babies, the evidence of smallpox and worse diseases,
the coma produced by opium—all these things are
such commonplaces that one almost ceases to observe
them.   But in my ideal Persia they must become a
matter, if necessary, for military law.   As a matter of
fact, I believe that the village dispensary, controlled
by a doctor or trained nurse, would be everywhere
welcomed and not resisted, judging by the way the

peasants throng round the foreigner, asking for
remedies; and judging also by the docility with which,
according to travellers such as Mrs. Bishop, instructions
are received. (Here is a vocation, I suggest, open to
many of our superfluous spinsters.) The unfortunate
Persian peasant, miles from any hospital or doctor, is
only too eager to be cured; otherwise he knows that
there is no hope for him but to have his nostrils stuffed
with herb-paste as he lies dying. But his faith is
childlike and unbounded; he will expect a cure for
blindness from birth, just as his wives will expect a
miraculous love-philtre: all foreigners are doctors, and
all doctors are omnipotent. With such material to
work upon, and the climate as an ally, the difficulty
should not be too great.

The structure grows: in an isolated, justly
administered Persia, we establish a population composed, so far as is humanly possible, of healthy-bodied
men. Still, they are ignorant. It is true that they
no longer wash their dead in the streams that presently
will fill their drinking-cups; they no longer imprison
their young in swaddling bands that during the course
of weeks and even months will receive all the excreta
of the body; they no longer drink water which has
absorbed a verse of the Koran as a cure for malaria;
but it is through fear of the law that they refrain from
doing these things, and not through any under-
standing in their own minds. They may do what
they are told to do—but they have not the most
elementary idea of why they do it. The question of
education rears its controversial head. Is education

to be attempted in this ideal State, or is it not? I think not. We in Europe are in a different position; we cannot, and would not, arrest a system which has already been set working, and our only aim should be to carry it forward to a greater and even greater perfection. In Persia—though in the cities there are schools [1]—the wheels have not yet begun to revolve so quickly that we could not bring them to a standstill by a touch of the hand. In education there should be no half-measures: either let it be complete, or let it be *nil*. Or let it be both; but complete in the one category, *nil* in the other. This gives rise to two instant objections: that one category includes all the rich, the other all the poor; and that potential intelligence among the poor will be lost owing to lack of opportunity. I confess that I cannot see how this last objection—the more important of the two—is to be overcome, unless we are to adapt Plato's system of guardians; but not quite in the sense that Plato meant it, for he was talking of soldiers—strong, swift, and brave; high-spirited but gentle; and endowed with a taste for philosophy, a kind of overseers of the intelligence on the look-out for natural genius, hard to imagine in a Persian village. It seems that we must take the risk, and let the tillers of the soil merely till the soil, without mixing themselves up in speculations dangerous to the half-trained mind. An anti-democratic creed, but the only possible one in dealing with a primitive community. Men do not miss what they

[1] In 1925, 91,190 students of both sexes were enrolled in the schools, of which 22,660 were in Teheran.

have never known, and if we, the more enlightened, confer upon them, in the first instance, practical advantages which will bear fruit only in the second or third generation, and let education wait, they have no business to complain. Moreover, the nature of the Persian peasant is, in this, on our side, for he is, to start with, of a contented disposition. " The inhabitants" (of a village near Isfahan), says an American cadastral report, " are penurious, credulous, and satisfied."   And again, " There is little crime or disorder." Whether it is humanly justifiable to take advantage of another man's simplicity and docility, and to keep him in a benighted condition because he is thereby more easily managed, is a question entirely for the conscience. My own view is, that it is justifiable, provided that those set in authority over him are truly sagacious and trustworthy—a large provision, I admit. Then finance, after all—for this ideal State is erected on a practical foundation—must be considered; and the drain upon our exchequer is already lavish.   But even apart from finance, and assuming that our ideal State is furnished with an ideal gold mine, education can wait, or even be put aside altogether. So we get government of the ignorant by the enlightened, with the line between the two sharply drawn. We get an agricultural and pastoral nation, almost entirely excluded from the outside world; a Paradise of six hundred thousand square miles with a population of ten millions, unique upon the face of the earth.

Ay me, I fondly dream. So strange a thicket has grown up round men's minds that the view over the sane and sunlit plains is obscured. Progress has come to be accepted as desirable, but any estimate of what progress really means is left entirely out of the reckoning. The acquisition of wealth, the spirit of competition, the desire for domination—to such idols do we sacrifice our souls. " Why, when God's earth is so wide," said Jalaluddin Rumi, " have you fallen asleep in a prison? Avoid entangled thoughts, that you may see the explanation in Paradise."

XX

Our last day. It set off with a flourish, up the Murdafil valley, rocky, and rich with oleander and pomegranate, but presently we came down into more nondescript country, where the smell of sulphur filled the air, and where we had to ford the same river, the Tembih, at least ten times. It was very hot—almost too hot—our hands by the end of the day were as brown as our shoes; the mules splashed gratefully through the water. We travelled with the whole caravan, contrary to our custom, for the way was tricky to find, and in this open, grassy country, the track had ceased to exist. We were travelling round the flank of the great grey Asmari mountain which lay like a stranded whale on our left. The hot sun and the level easiness of the going made us all rather listless; the mules jangled their bells fretfully, and continually flicked at the flies with their ears and tails; ahead of us the black plume of smoke rose unwavering into the sky; we felt that all our interest had been left in those hills and valleys which had closed up for ever behind us, inviolate now save for the crawling stream of the tribes, as indigenous and as inevitable as the eagles and the ibex. Still, one must admit that the full caravan made a pretty sight, whether the pack mules ranged out freely over the grass, or strung themselves in a file to wade through the bright, shallow river. It made me tired to think that those mules, arrived at the oil-fields, would load up with petrol, and turning round, set off again on the same weary way, back to Isfahan, up and down the Road, till they dropped and were eaten by the vultures.

That last day's stage was shorter than usual, and by four o'clock we were encamped for the last time. We had hated our tents, Heaven knows, when the floor had been muddy and the nights cold, but now at Gurghir, where it was warm and dry, on the grassy plain, we were overcome by a sentimental regret. It was now that Copley Amory produced the surprise which he had been saving up in secret in that inexhaustible wooden box of his: a bottle of champagne. The champagne was quite warm, and we had no ice; nor did a single bottle admit of a very generous allowance among five people; but we had touched no wine since our jeroboam smashed at Do-Pulan, and that single, tepid, jealously measured draught put a livelier spirit into us than all the poured-out sparkle in London. All honour to Copley Amory and his kind heart. Throughout the journey he had hovered, tactful, sympathetic, and unobtrusive. When we had seen him, deep in his confabulations with Rahim, we had been forced to smile, whatever our state of irritability. We had smiled again whenever we saw him riding along, notebook in hand—what was he writing in that notebook?—reins hanging loose, oblivious to ascent or

descent, a flower stuck in his hat, his gaunt red mule
doing the work for him, his legs dangling, having lost
the stirrup; half Don Quixote, half Canterbury Pil-
grim. He had said very little, but he had imposed
good humour on the party. And now he crowned it
all with a bottle of champagne.

We drank it hilariously, on the plain of Gurghir,
keeping meanwhile a rather nervous eye on the much-
ornamented camp which stood on a rise just above our
own camp. This, we knew, had been prepared for
Sardar Zaffar, the Il-Khani, who had been the guest
of the Company at the oil-fields, and whose arrival was
expected at any moment. We had groaned inwardly
when we saw his tents, for we knew that meant a
pasirayi, but some slight hope remained that it might
be deferred until the following morning. Presently,
however, we saw the distant beam of headlights sweep
over the darkening plain: the Il-Khani was arriving in
the motors of the Company. Civilisation and the wild
were meeting. We had almost forgotten that motors
existed, but here they were, transporting the all but
royal chief of the nomad tribes. We watched him
walk from the cars to his camp, a dumpy round figure
in the white *kolah* of the Bakhtiari and a biscuit-coloured
robe, followed by a trail of officers, servants, and
guards armed with rifles. We saw the procession go
up the rise and enter the camp.

We had tidied ourselves as well as we could, in
expectation of the inevitable summons, which was
quickly brought by a dapper little Persian officer.
Would we do the Il-Khani the honour of a visit? We

accordingly followed the officer, jumping the stream
which divided the Il-Khani's camp from ours, and
after climbing the knoll found Sardar Zaffar capaciously
seated on a very small chair in the midst of his attend-
ants. Two slender Bakhtiari guards stood behind him,
leaning on their rifles; a group of white-robed Bakhtiari lounged near by, holding their horses, illuminated
by the flaring torches. Down in the dip the head-lights
of the cars streamed out over the plain. This was truly
Persia,—this mixture of the modern and the romantic.

The Il-Khani was extremely gracious. We were
able to tell him that we had met his son, and as my
memory revived of that gallant figure reining up his
horse I wondered what precise spot in the mountains
saw him that night, beyond Shalil, beyond Do-Pulan?
The Il-Khani sighed over Persian politics as he drank
his tea and knocked the ash off his cigarette. The
little officer who had come to fetch us was very eager
to display his English. The lounging Bakhtiari
watched us with a kind of inquisitive contempt in their
fine dark eyes. Night fell, complete; and more
candles were brought, and more tea in glasses. We
said at last that we were tired, and begged now to be
excused. The Il-Khani offered me the string of corals
with which he was playing, slipping the beads between
his fingers as he talked, as all Persians do; it lies on
my table as I write.

After we had got back to our camp he sent us
presents out of his store: tinned peaches and tinned
asparagus. Our table looked like the counter of an
English grocer under the stars of Gurghir.

XXI

We were greeted next morning by the familiar sight of the mules standing ready to be loaded, tossing their bells and flicking at the flies, but for us there was no more trekking with the caravan. The Mouse looked at me reproachfully as she stood waiting with my saddle on her back, and the orange saddle-cloth, and my blue-and-white saddle-bag slung across her rump; or I imagined that she did, but perhaps she was really glad to get rid of me and to return into the keeping of Hossein. The caravan was to go by road, but we five were to go in two of the motors which had brought the Il-Khani. Black tents sprinkled the plain,—the last that we were to see of the nomads. It was civilisation in the most violent contrast that lay ahead.

The black plume of smoke that we had seen from above Malamir had by now reproduced itself in many smaller plumes which hung threatening in the sky. For some way we travelled over the grass, bumping and bouncing till our heads hit the hoods and the springs grated with every jerk of the motor. But we were coming to the edge of the plain, and as the foot-hills began to rise we found ourselves in a most extraordinary landscape; the landscape characteristic, as we were to learn, of the oil-fields. We crept between hills comparable only to the cardboard hills of a scenic railway, creased, bleached, altogether fantastic. Still, there was no evidence of man's occupation, save in the hanging feathers of smoke. We might have been in some strange forsaken part of the world, breaking our way through a pathless region.

Pathless region! What is this? A tarred road!

The tyres of the motor ran suddenly and smoothly on a perfect surface. An English highway. What lay at the end of it? York? Cambridge? No, Sheffield rather; look at the smoke trailing out across the sky. An English highway, leading, so it seemed, straight into hell. A perfect motor road, running between those strange crumpled hillocks.

We came to a tent, with white rough-cast gatch floor, and the inevitable, pathetic, English attempt at a garden round it. We went in: a man's sitting-room; the *Royal Magazine*; pipes; P. G. Wodehouse; and, most startling sight of all, a telephone. No sign of the owner. Harold Nicolson picked up the receiver, and a prompt voice said, "Number, please." A cross-connection cut in; he heard a man's voice saying irritably, "I can't think where they've got to; they were due to-day; Balfour has been out scouring the country for them all morning." "Hallo. This is Nicolson speaking. . . . I've forgotten", he said, turning to us, "how to use the telephone."

XXII

But we were very definitely in the world of the telephone,—very definitely, and with staggering sudden-
ness, in the world of every mechanical invention. To
those who arrive at the oil-fields in the ordinary way,
coming up from the tankers and gasometers of Abadan,
there is, no doubt, nothing very surprising in this
perfectly organised, clanking, belching settlement; but
we had come straight out of the wilds into a circle
dependent entirely upon the horrible resources of
modern ingenuity. The contrast was so great as to
produce an almost physical shock. Those days in the
mountains had stretched themselves out into a complete lifetime,—twelve days? twelve years, rather;—
the mind had adapted itself to those conditions; now
it had to be slewed round in the space of half an hour;
it had to readjust itself, to remember all the forgotten
lessons, to take again for granted all the standards
against which it had, with relief, rebelled. From
constant contact with life reduced to its simplest
elements, we walked straight into a hell of civilisation.
Nothing was lacking, as we were to learn, from blast
furnaces down to lathes adjusted to the fraction of
an inch. Here, you could get a boiler made or your

spectacles repaired.   You could plunge a drill for a
mile down into the soil of Persia.   Rocks were ground
to powder, and ranged in little glass phials.   There
were grocers' shops with the familiar tins and bottles on
the counters; there were schools, and cool, organised
hospitals; there were tennis-courts occupied by young
women in summer dresses and young men in white
flannels.   There was, no doubt, society, intrigues, and
gossip.   One shuddered at the thought of it.   A heavy
smell of gas pervaded everything; at certain points
along the road barriers were erected, where all matches
were taken away, to be restored further on; the traffic
was controlled by police in white ducks; buses ran;
the black tarred roads swept up and down in switchback between white bungalows.   The roads swept up
and down,—for this colony lay, not in the English
midlands, but plumped down amongst the fantastic,
the almost grotesque, scenery of the Persian oil-fields.

To give any idea, in words, of this landscape is
extremely difficult.   The hills were not high, but so
curiously crinkled, and of so strange a colour, now
brown, now green, that in their singularity they might
well have been upon another planet.   Like the cardboard hills of a scenic railway to which I have already
compared them—and find myself coming back to the
comparison for want of a better—they also resembled
the hills on a raised physical map; miniature ranges,
with the creases disproportionately noticeable.   Left
to itself, the landscape would have been queer enough;
but with the introduction of mechanical structures it
turned into a nightmare world.   Huge skeletons,

looking like a schoolboy's model made out of Meccano,
reared themselves in unexpected places; and a large
initial letter in black paint on white indicated the
well. You remember the hundreds of tins of petrol
which you have seen or used in England, those tins
with their screw-caps so awkward to open unless you
have a second tin to do it with, and you prepare with
some interest to see your old friend petrol in its natural
state. B.P.; Palm Oil; the familiar signs return to
your memory. But you will be disappointed. More
than a hundred wells are working over an area of
fifty square miles, producing their four and a half
million tons of oil a year; but of the oil itself one
sees never a drop. Secrecy seems to attend the
mysterious business of dragging it up from its lair;
one sees the head of the well, one hears the murmur
of voices, but of the results one sees nothing at all.
The conduits are closed and sealed. In a great pipe-
line that writhes over the strange hills, and down
into the corn-clad plains of Arabistan, the glutinous
treasure of Maidan-i-Naftun is carried away to Abadan
and the sea.

There are other wells in process of construction.
Down there,—sometimes even a mile down,—the
nose of the drill probes and bores in a conflict never
beheld by mortal eyes. A narrow, pointed enemy, the
drill pierces its way inch by inch through the buried
rock, and the only visible result of its subterranean
operations comes to the surface in a constant stream
of dirty water and occasionally a few specimen
chips of stone; only a stream of dirty water and a

handful of chips to indicate the meeting of two such
protagonists as the secret foundations of the earth
and the greedy, inquisitive importunities of man.
Down there they wrestle, and man wins; the all-but
immovable mass crumbles, finally, before the irresist-
ible force. A grinding patience is at work; the rock
spreads in wide and ancient formation; the engine of
man comes stabbing down, through the darkness of
the earth, a sharp and persistent auger. Up at the top,
in the shelter of the rig, the machinery clanks through
the long, hot hours, monotonously; a few Persians sit
about; a young Englishman, grimy in shirt and shorts,
rouses himself from his apathy to give a few explanations to the strangers. " Put your hand here ", he
says, " and you'll feel the vibration." You put your
hand on the chain, as he tells you, and the vibration
of a thump comes up to your fingers from the battle
going on down there in the bowels of the earth. But
it is the vibration of a thump which happened eight
minutes ago. Outside, the sun is scorching; sun-
helmets are already necessary, yet the month is only
April. You are appalled by the thought that this work
will continue all through the summer: if this is April,
what will the temperature be in June, in July, in
August? This is one of the hottest places in the
world; the temperature rises to 126° Fahrenheit, and
stays there from May to October, with the added
horror of a damp wind in September; yet through it
all the work never slacks off. You thank the young
Englishman; he nods, in the indifferent, off-hand
manner which all connection with machinery seems to

beget,—you are reminded of the manner of young men in garages at home. You go out into the blazing sun, leaving him to his vigil in the dirty rig among the Persians; leaving him there to the days which will grow steadily hotter and hotter, while the drill noses its way down, and the chemists in the laboratory examine the specimens of rock brought up, lest the drill should suddenly plunge through into the limestone and a fountain of oil should shoot up into the rig, uncontrolled, drenching the men and suffocating them with subterranean gases. When this dramatic moment is believed to be near at hand, a notice appears as a warning to those approaching the well. Terse and severe, it says: " No smoking. Drilling in Main Limestone."

How the oil got there, or what oil actually is, remains an enigma for geologists and chemists. Is it the product of buried forests, or of marine organisms and seaweed strewn on rocks which were once the bed of a vanished ocean? Did trees or did millions of fish perish to light our boarding-houses and drive our motors? Nobody knows for certain. Millions of fish, —in this world of doubt one thing at least seems to be beyond dispute: the quantity of fish that have been spawned since the beginning of life. We have grown accustomed to the idea that for our own chalk cliffs and the atolls of the South Seas these brisk and multitudinous organisms were responsible; now it seems that we must credit them also with the world's supply of petrol. How many decomposed fish go to one gallon of petrol? How many roes, spines, and gills do we burn in one hour of gas? One fact at any rate is known about oil even by the most ignorant, and that is that it will not mix with water. To this fact it owed its recognition as early as the days of Herodotus, and became a useful commodity in the ancient civilisations of China and Japan; for this reason it was known to the Bakhtiari, who, finding it afloat on the puddles, skimmed it off, and used the oil to smear on their sores and wounds, and traded in its deposit of pitch with the Arabs to caulk the seams of boats on the Tigris and Euphrates. Its properties as fuel were likewise known to the Zoroastrians, the ruins of whose Temple of Fire stand to this day among the wells and derricks of the Company. On how small a chance does notoriety depend! Had oil been of a more accommodating nature,—had it, in fact, mixed with the water in those miniature craters which received its seepage,—William Knox d'Arcy might never have heard the legend of its presence in a lonely valley of the Bakhtiari hills.

Just as oil is the last thing visible to those who visit, and even to those who live in, the Persian oil-fields, so do the activities of the settlement appear to be concerned with many things unconnected with the getting of oil. I assume that they all really conspire to the same end; but the advantage of visiting such a place in complete ignorance, without even the most elementary technical knowledge, is that one enters a new world of complicated mystery, much as an ant, with the ultimate idea of government in mind, might observe the intricacies of party politics. This is an oil-field, but I see no oil; I see instead vast hangars full of boilers and furnaces, pistons and driving-rods, lathes and leather belts, all glowing and thumping and whirling, stoked and controlled by dark half-naked men with shovels or oil-cans—actually!—in their hands, lifting lumps of red-hot metal on to anvils, striking them with hammers and making the sparks fly, running with red amorphous masses clipped in giant pincers, setting in motion a tangle of machinery which will cut a round hole in iron as though the iron were butter,—and all in the pursuit of that clandestine deposit of trees, seaweed, or fish. Very odd. And all to send ships across the sea, or motors to course up and down the roads, or aeroplanes to draw a line across the sky.

These sheds, these belching monsters of crude power, these instruments of strong precision, filled me with an innocent wonder. Not the least remarkable thing was, that they should be worked by Persians and Indians who could probably neither read nor write. What in heaven's name did these simple creatures make of the engines of industry? What was their general conception, for instance, of the current of electricity which they could arouse by pulling over a lever? They knew their own particular fraction of the work they had been taught, but what possible conception could they have of the whole? What, in their imagination, was the world which their labour helped to feed? Did they ever trouble about anything which lay beyond the scope of their own immediate concern? And who was I, littered with so many inexact smatterings of information, to wonder at them, who at least were trained to beat a lump of metal into shape?

But I realised then that few things can be more suggestive to the lay mind than machinery on a grand scale. This demon that we have let loose among us, however obedient and controlled, still retains its demoniacal properties. Its soul is made of fire and force; it performs its duties to the accompaniment of din and clangour, under the ever-present menace of strength compressed and withheld. It is a fiend; but a fiend not wholly of our own making; the elements existed, and all that we have done is to confine them into a prison of iron and steel. The very iron that we mould runs in a stream of molten liquid more terrible than fire. The uninitiated stand amazed, or should stand amazed, if they have any spark of awe within them, knowing not whether to wonder most at the magnificence of the elements or at the audacity of man. For if the very pigmies who labour, ignorant of all but the immediate work under their hands, can take on a heroic semblance in the glare of the furnace, what shall be said of the brain which conceives such arrogant things—creating, like the musician or the mathematician, a world out of bare and original material? Out of fire and force he creates his own symphonies and equations. But the musician and the mathematician move among such delicate morsels as notes and numbers, abstractions which now appear as existing solely in our imagination, now as enjoying the only absolute and independent reality; the maker of engines handles the explosive fiends of nature, and drives them along such channels as suit the purpose of his will.

At night we ascended a hill and stood looking down on the oil-field with its ruddy flares glowing in the darkness. The crumpled ranges were invisible, but our daylight acquaintance with them made their presence unforgettable; one could not really persuade oneself that one was looking down on an outspread town of industrial England; besides, such soft air as fanned our faces never rose from English soil; pleasantly warm, at that midnight in that month of April, the foreboding of the torrid summer was in it. Nevertheless, it required an effort to remember that one stood on a hill in Luristan, a hill designed by its geographical position to rise, one of many, in a region known only to a roving population, and which by the mere accident of a primordial vegetable or marine deposit had been rescued for exploitation out of that wild jumble of hills which constituted the domain of the Bakhtiari. This was indeed as much a part of the Bakhtiari territory, by right, as Qaleh Madrasseh or Agha Mihrab; yet, because fish had rotted miles beneath the surface the enterprise of the men of another continent had transfigured the landscape and forced it —how violently!—into another character. Twenty years ago this region lay inviolate; only the wandering shepherds bent to scoop the oil as it floated on the pools. Layard, could he return here to-day, would find some difficulty in identifying the place with his own description of it. " They (the ruins of Masjid-i-Suleiman) occur in a very wild district. I took advantage of the deserted state of the country to visit them." He would not find the country in a deserted state now. Below us in the valley stretched the long lines of road-lights, marking off the populous quarters; but the chief focus of light concentrated on the huge flares of burning gas, a glowing smear in the night, those flares whose smoke we had seen from the heights above Malamir. And as I stood there, my head full of the things I had seen that day, half-understood words and explanations jostling together and producing a sort of thunder of incomprehensible magnificence and audacity, the remembered solitudes of the Bakhtiari mountains rose up and swelled together with the energy of the oil-field into a vast, significant, and, as it were, symbolic symphony.

XXIII

I SEE now that although I started this book with little
hope of making it into anything more than the mere
record of an expedition, it has almost of its own accord
assumed a certain shape, and piled itself up into two
main blocks, ordained by the force of contrast. Two
different communities have crossed the stage; the one
weary, ignorant, and poor; the other energetic, scien-
tific, and prosperous; but both equally enslaved by
the habit of their different modes of thought. I wish
I could say that my impartiality had been such that
the reader is unable to tell which way my sympathies
lie. It seems fitting that it should conclude with yet
a third image—the representation neither of an ana-
chronistic existence nor of a modern civilisation. The
pastoral tribes have streamed by, simple survivals from
a lost world; the steam-hammers have thudded round
the site of what was once the Temple of Fire; now it
is time to see what becomes of empires as arrogant as
the British and, on so oracular a note, to end.

Persepolis is particularly suitable for such a purpose
—to stand midway between the Bakhtiari country and
the outposts of England as typified by the Anglo-
Persian Oil Company. It is suitable because, although

it was once the capital of the Persian Empire, its ruins now lie among surroundings as primitive as the plain of Malamir. The gaunt columns remain, thrusting up at the sky, but of the site of the city of Istakhr there is nothing but the nibbled grass. Persepolis gains in splendour from its isolation. Not another building stands anywhere near it; not a hut, not a guard-house, not a shepherd's shelter; only the vast green plain, encircled by mountains and the open sky and the hawks that wheel and hover between the columns. As a ship launching out on an expanse of sea, the great terrace drives forward on to the plain, breasting it, the columns rising like naked spars into the clear blue of the sky. At first sight it may seem smaller than one had expected to find it, but that is due to the immensity of the plain and to the mass of the hill against which it is pushed up. The terrace, in fact, juts squarely out, backing against the hill as though for defence; but the effect is less of a seeking for defence than of an imperial launching of defiance, a looking-out across the plain, a raised domination above the level ground: the throne of kings over-hanging the dwellings of the people. But the dwell-ings of the people which once spread over the plain have disappeared, and nothing of the royal capital remains but the ruins that were once the citadel of Xerxes and Darius; the dwellings of the people, no doubt, were made of wattle and sun-dried bricks, ephemeral material, whereas the kings glorified them-selves in stone. A thousand years, I suppose, will level the disparity between them. The propylaea of

Xerxes, the palace of Darius, will have enjoyed a few thousand more years of survival than sun-baked bazaars which sheltered the potter and the barber.

So stands Persepolis, looking out over the deserted plain. The space, the sky, the hawks, the raised-up eminence of the terrace, the quality of the Persian light, all give to the great terrace a sort of springing airiness, a sort of treble, to which the massive structure of bastion and archways plays a corrective bass. It is only when you draw near that you realise how massive that structure really is. It has all the weight of the Egyptian temples; square, monolithic. The terrace itself is supported on enormous blocks, its angles casting square shadows; a double stairway climbs it, a stairway that at its landing-place is superbly dominated by huge winged bulls. Now you are in the midst of the ruins: the columns soar, supporting no roof; square doorways open, leading into no halls. (But see, within the jamb of one doorway is carved a king wrestling with a lion, and within another a king stepping forward under the shade of a parasol; these were the kings that ruled, but here, following the easy rise of steps, comes a procession of captive kings.) A little further, and you are in the Hall of the Hundred Columns, a wilderness of tumbled ruins, but ruins which in their broken detail testify to the richness of the order that once was here: fallen capitals; fragments of carving small enough to go into a pocket, but whorled with the curls of an Assyrian beard; wars and dynasties roll their forgotten drums, as the fragment is balanced for a moment in the palm of the hand.

Over this roofless desolation hangs the sun, cutting black square shadows, striking a carving into sharper relief; and silence reigns, but for the dry-leaf scurry of a lizard over the stones.   This hall was roofed with cedar, says Quintus Curtius; and now the discovered ashes of carbonised cedar corroborate the account of the historians: this hall of Darius flamed indeed beneath the vengeance of Alexander.   Little did it avail Darius that he should have caused the *Avesta* to be written in letters of gold and silver on twelve thousand tanned ox-hides.

The hand of man has never desecrated these ruins, no excavator's pick has ever rung upon these stones; tumbled and desolate they lie to-day, as they lay after the might of Alexander had pushed them over.   The heat of the Persian summers has passed over them and bleached them; they have flushed in the light of many sunrises and bared themselves to the silver of many moons; the wild flowers have sown themselves in the crevices and the lizards scurry over the pavements; but it is a dead world, as befits the sepulchre of an imperial race.

Ruined cities.   Ranging away from Persepolis, I remember other wrecks of pride, splendour, and majesty: the ziggurat of Ur against the sunset, the undulating mounds that were Babylon, the gay broken colonnades of Palmyra.   Golden, graceful, airy, debased, Palmyra rises like a flower from the desert in an oasis of palms and apricots.   At the apex of a flattened and irregular triangle between Damascus and Baghdad, Palmyra lies on the old caravan route, and the strings of camels still slouch beneath the triumphal arches of Zenobia and Odenathus. But the Street of the Hundred Columns is now nothing but a transparent screen of pillars, framing the desert, and in the precincts of the Temple of Baal clusters an Arab village, the squalid houses incongruously put together with the stones of the once magnificent centre of a pagan faith. What is Palmyra now? Where is the glory of Solomon who built Tadmor in the wilderness? A few tourists motor out from Beirut, and the desert traffic of camel caravans passes through on its leisurely way. The Arab children squabble in the gutters. There is a French *poste de police*. There is a derelict building, originally designed as an hotel. But now that even the Trans-Desert Mail no longer takes Palmyra in its rush—as it did when the Druses terrorised the southern route—it seems likely that Palmyra will return to the isolation to which it is geographically destined, and that the flush of its prosperity under the Roman Empire will resemble the flush of flowers over the desert in spring,—with this difference, that spring for Palmyra is not recurrent. It happened once, and will not happen again; a miracle the more exquisite for its singleness and fugacity.

You come upon Palmyra unexpectedly, if you approach it from the Damascus side, going through a gorge crowned by Turkish forts, and coming out on to a full view of the desert with these surprising ruins standing in the white, pale sand. Lovely in colour, as golden as honey, the vistas of columns and arches give Palmyra a lacy quality: it is a series of frames, and nothing so much enhances the beauty of landscape as to be framed in a fragment of architecture. But on looking closer this architecture presents a puzzle: it is Roman, surely? but there is something not quite Roman about it; there are mistakes that the Roman builders would not have made. Indeed, the Romans did not build it, no; Arabs built it, dazzled by what they had seen or heard of the Roman models. Most people criticise Palmyra on this account. Certainly it is neither as pure nor as majestic as Baalbec. It lacks the grand solidity of Roman building, and the Roman sense of proportion is notably absent. But I like Palmyra. It is very feminine; it is gay, whimsical, and a little meretricious. It seems to have drunk the desert sun, and to have granted free passage to all the desert winds with a wanton insouciance. Palmyra is a Bedouin girl laughing because she is dressed up as a Roman lady.

And there, lastly, under the snows of Lebanon lie the mighty ruins of Heliopolis. The Temple of Bacchus retains its shape, but of the Temple of Jupiter only six columns survive out of the original fifty-four. Baalbec had its worthy enemies: Genghiz, Timur, and Saladin; besides the earthquakes which have crashed pediment and capital to the ground. There lie the blocks of masonry, here gapes a vault; here is a column, propping itself against the wall of the Temple. It is a wilderness of masonry; havoc such as might have been wrought in a sudden onslaught by the anger of the very god to whom the greatest temple was dedicated, that Jupiter who at Baalbec was called Baal,

—not the hirsute Jove of the Romans, but a beardless god, covered with scales, and holding in one hand a scourge, and in the other, lightning and ears of corn. Baalbec has gone the way of those cities of antiquity on whose ruin no later city has arisen. True, a little town has grown up beside it, so that it enjoys neither the superb isolation of Persepolis nor the native sprinkling of Palmyra, but the little town is insignificant, and it is really the wreck of Heliopolis which dominates the lovely valley between Lebanon and Anti-Lebanon.

There is another difference between Baalbec and those two other cities. The plain of Persepolis is green indeed with the short grass, and at Palmyra the fruit trees of the oasis foam with blossom in the spring, but there is no sign of cultivation anywhere. Round Baalbec the fertile land is carefully tilled; the permanence of agriculture, that detailed, laborious, and persistent craft, is nowhere more strongly emphasised than here, where it pursues its quiet way undisturbed by the presence of a crumbled civilisation. It seems not irrelevant to wonder whether in the course of centuries the Anglo-Persian oil-fields may not revert to the solitudes of the Bakhtiari hills, while London, Paris, and New York lie with the wild flowers blowing over their stones, and fields of corn bend to the breeze for the bread of the population in some distant capital whose name we do not yet know.

APPENDIX

NOTES ON DISTANCES, CAMPING-GROUNDS, ETC.

Contributed by Gladwyn Jebb

THE altitudes are mostly taken from the report of Captain H. E. Wells, who went on a surveying tour in 1881, and a few from H. B. Lynch.

ISFAHAN—SHALAMZAR, 9-10 hours (by car).

Road fairly good, except through villages. Guide available. Excellent *amarat* at Shalamzar. Height at Shalamzar, 6743 feet.

SHALAMZAR—NAGHAN, 4½ hours.

Top of Zirreh Pass reached in two hours. Steep descent to plateau. Then easy going until the final short (but steep) descent to Naghan. Good *amarat*. Height at Naghan, 6480 feet.

NAGHAN—DO-PULAN, 5½ hours.

Road crosses the Ab-i-Sabz-i-Kuh. Thence fairly good to the top of the pass and a long and wearisome descent to Do-Pulan. Very little camping-space. What there is, is mostly wheat fields. Small village and *chaikhaneh*. Height at Do-Pulan, 4950 feet.

Do-Pulan—Gandom Kar, 6 hours.

Very long pull up the Barreh Murdeh. Slimy mud and rocks. Fairly easy descent to Gandom Kar. Quite good camping-ground. A few huts and a *chaikhaneh*.

Gandom Kar—Shalil, 8 hours.

Take upper road (see Note) after entering ravine. Sarkhun (good camping-ground, reached in three hours). Going fairly easy to Shalil. (Caravanserai.) Inferior camping-ground in rocks near caravanserai. A long day.

Shalil—Deh Diz, 5½ hours.

Road crosses the Bazuft (good camping-ground). Very long and steep rocky climb up the Murvarid Pass. Easy descent to Deh Diz. Excellent camping-ground in a pomegranate grove on left of road just before entering village. Height at Deh Diz, 5221 feet.

Deh Diz—Qaleh Madrasseh, 7 hours.

Easy road to Pul-i-Godar (five hours). *Chaikhaneh* on bridge. Good camping-ground. Fairly good road (uphill) to Qaleh Madrasseh. (Ruined caravanserai, first-rate grassy camping-ground.) Height at Pul-i-Godar, 2320 feet.

Qaleh Madrasseh—Malamir, 7 hours.

About one and a half hours to top of the Gardan-i-Sarrak (rather rough going). Descent to the plain of Malamir (last bit stony). Easy going over the plain, road apt to be marshy and flooded in spring. Dirty village (*chaikhaneh*). Best camping-ground near a caravanserai about a mile beyond the village. Height at Malamir, 2930 feet.

MALAMIR—AGHA MIHRAB, 6½ hours.

Road leads S. for about five miles to Halagun (ruins and huts), then due W. over rolling plain to the Imam Zadeh of Sheikh Nasrullah (caravanserai) camping-ground. Road continues W. for some four miles over a low pass (rocky road) descending to the Ab-i-Murgah. After five and a half hours the caravanserai (half ruined) of Murdafil (camping-ground). Road leaves the Murgah and ascends the Murdafil Pass to the S.W. Excellent camping-ground at Agha Mihrab.

AGHA MIHRAB—GURGHIR, 8 hours.

Top of Murdafil Pass reached in about an hour. Long and weary descent on the other side, though easy going on the whole. Road follows the stream down until eventually the Tembih river is reached passing another Qaleh Madrasseh (caravanserai, camping-ground). Follows the Tembih river round the bottom of the Asmari mountain, then branches off to the S. to the camping-ground of Gurghir. A long (and hot) day. Height at Gurghir, 1480 feet.

GURGHIR—MAIDAN-I-NAFTUN, 2 hours (by car).

Track to Yamaha. Made roads thence to Fields.

The following distances are given by H. B. Lynch:

Malamir to Gurghir, 26 miles.
Do-Pulan to Malamir, 75½ miles.
Pul-i-Godar to Malamir, 22¾ miles.
Deh Diz to Pul-i-Godar, 11½ miles.

NOTE.—Travellers who are apt to precede their caravan in a fury of impatience, or linger behind owing to inexperience or sloth, may find themselves, after leaving Gandom Kar, enjoying the experience of being lost in the Bakhtiari mountains.   This is due to the fact that there are two quite distinct roads between this place and Shalil, which diverge at the end of a ravine about a mile below Gandom Kar.   The right-hand fork crosses the stream and follows it down the valley.   In bad weather, or when the stream is very full, it is impassable.   After about one and a half hours this road leaves the stream and climbs steeply (very muddy and slippery after rain) to Gumish Su (*chaikhaneh* and a few huts in a narrow valley).   The left-hand fork climbs steeply up for about 600 feet, then follows the top of the ravine, eventually entering another ravine (? Hazar Jerib, but this name is not known locally).   At the end of this ravine is Sarkhun, which may equally be reached by the other road if one does not turn up the hill to Gumish Su.   This left-hand fork is the regular Bakhtiari road, and should be used by laden mules except in very good weather.   After a ford at Sarkhun the road winds up the mountain to the right, passing Gumish Su about 500 feet below on the right, and continues to Shalil.

G. J.

BIBLIOGRAPHY

Persia and the Persian Question, chap. xxiv.: Lord Curzon.

Journal of the R.G.S., vol. ix.: article by Sir H. Rawlinson, 1836.

Travels in Luristan: Baron C. A. de Bode, 1841.

Journeys in Persia: Mrs. Bishop, 1890.

Early Adventures in Persia, Susiana, and Babylonia, including a Residence among the Bakhtiari and other wild Tribes: Sir Henry Layard, 1887.

Six Months in Persia, vol. ii.: E. Stack.

Proceedings of the Royal Geographical Society, new series, vols. v. and xii. *Surveying Tours in Southern Persia*, by Captain H. E. Wells, 1881. *The Karun River*, by the Hon. G. Curzon, 1890. *Across Luristan to Isfahan*, by H. B. Lynch.

Journal of the Royal Geographical Society, vols. xii. and xvi. *Ancient Sites among the Bakhtiari Mountains*, by Prof. Long. *A Description of the Province of Khuzistan*, by A. H. Layard.

Fifteen Months' Pilgrimage through Untrodden Tracks of Khuzistan and Persia: J. H. Stocqueler, 1832.